Killing Kate

A Story of Turning
Abuse and Tragedy into
Transformation and Triumph

Kate Ranta with Alisa Divine

Personal Power Press, Inc.

Bay City, Michigan

Killing Kate

A Story of Turning Abuse and Tragedy into
Transformation and Triumph

© 2019 Kate Ranta, Alisa Divine and Personal Power Press

Library of Congress Catalogue Card Number: 2019937105

ISBN: 978-0-9821568-8-9

Printed in the United States of America

Personal Power Press, Inc.
Bay City, MI 48706

Cover Photography By:
Alisa Divine, www.alisadivine.com

Cover Design By:
Parker Haller, parkerhaller72@gmail.com

Disclaimer: The authors and publisher have utilized their best
efforts in preparing the information in this book. The stories in this
book are experiences and recollections. Some names were changed
to protect the privacy of individuals.

This book is dedicated to:
my parents, Robert and Susan Ranta,
my sons, Henry and William,
and to the countless women
who've lost their voices
at the hands of abusive partners.

Table of Contents

Foreword

By Evan Rachel Wood

If there is one thing Voldemort cannot understand, it's love. He didn't realize that love as powerful as your mother's for you, leaves its own mark. Not a scar, no visible sign...to have been loved so deeply, even though the person who loved us is gone, will give us some protection forever. ~Albus Dumbledore

Although this quote is from Harry Potter, its meaning holds much truth. Especially when I think of Kate.

I met Kate in Sacramento just a day before we would storm the Capitol building in hopes of passing a new law in California called "The Phoenix Act." It would ensure more rights for domestic violence victims.

A handful of domestic violence survivors, including myself, sat together and shared our most intimate and gut wrenching stories to prepare for our day ahead. I was struck immediately by Kate and her young son. Her story moved me to tears. Kate's act of protection over her family rang true for many of us, especially ones with small children.

Most parents will tell you, when your child is in danger, you don't think, you act.

Even if it means making the ultimate sacrifice. You will keep your family safe, at all cost.

But Kate's love hasn't stopped there.

Kate's act of bravery has taken on a life of its own now.

Her story is the force that holds the door shut, keeping evil at bay, in hopes of protecting us all.

Domestic violence affects everyone in some form or another — whether it happens to us, or someone we love. The problem is a world-wide epidemic that is grossly overlooked. On average, nearly 20 people per minute are physically abused by an intimate partner in the United States alone. During one year, that equates to more than 10 million women and men. The presence of a gun in a domestic violence situation increases the risk of homicide by 500 percent.

Kate travels the country, speaking truth to power and educating people about DV and gun violence. She doesn't have to do this, but the choice to be seen and dedicate her life to the protection of others is something to not only be grateful for, but also a good reason to respect her. The more we listen, the more we heal; the more we can move progress.

Stories like Kate's live on and pave the way for all of us to lead safer and happier lives, free of fear and free of shame. They teach us how to turn pain into power and how to not only survive, but to come back to life. They teach us that love can be the greatest weapon any of us has.

I am grateful to know Kate and inspired by the relentless quest she is on to make sure that what happened to her and her family never happens to anyone else. It shows people that domestic violence is not as cut and dry as some would like to believe and that even when you do everything you are "supposed to" the system is still flawed, and this fight is far from over.

Because of the survivors who came together in Sacramento that day, the law passed through the Senate unanimously. Proving that we can move mountains when we stand by one another.

By all of us standing up to hold the door closed, we can open a new one.

Together.

Evan Rachel Wood
Across The Universe, Westworld, Thirteen, and The Wrestler

Introduction

By Lovern Gordon

As a child witness and adult survivor of domestic violence, it's not difficult to connect to the truth of my friend's story. The horrific day that forever changed Kate and her family's lives is the horrific reality many live every day.

It's essentially how we became connected…sharing our "knowledge" about the abuse we both encountered for a *Huffington Post* feature. Though our stories were different with very diverse outcomes, there were similarities in the buildup that defined us as "survivor sisters." We didn't ask for or seek out such a bond. But the death of who we once were from the abuse we suffered, strongly connected us.

Kate's story gives voice to those who are stuck in the secrecy of an abusive relationship. They may be victims who relent on the many reasons why they should leave, victims with children who witness the attacks, bystanders who can sometimes even become victims. Those who survive can choose to be the light that no one would suspect could ever come out from the darkness. To be able to evolve from victim to survivor is no easy task.

As you delve into the circumstances that took Kate there and walk a mile in her shoes, it's my hope you know that your voice is just as important as hers on this issue. There are so many waiting for your permission to speak up. As bystanders, who among you can use your understanding, open-mindedness and awareness as it relates to this issue? As victims or survivors, how are you going to use Kate's death that day to propel you into rebirth?

Your Survivor Sister,

Lovern Gordon
President of Love Life Now Foundation, Inc.
www.lovelifenow.org

Killing Kate

I was meeting Kate Ranta in Alexandria, Virginia when she agreed to be a participant in the book I was writing #SheWins — a collection of short stories and portraiture of domestic abuse survivors. I was in search of women who were ready to talk about their experiences. I contacted her knowing she received a lot of media attention for her activist and advocacy work around the country. It was going to be a simple visit. A series of photos and then details about her experience that I could use for my book. I was looking forward to meeting her....

I already knew Kate's story was shocking. After the photos were taken we sat down to talk. There were still many questions I wanted to ask her. What were the warning signs she saw — and how much did she suffer at his hands?

"Kate, how did he NOT kill you? How did you escape?"

She began...

Chapter 1
My Only Choice
Was To Leave

Or — at least try to leave.

I got up, staggered through the front door, took a few steps on the grass and my legs turned to liquid. I collapsed. Like a drunk walk. Not the fun kind of drunk, when you're out with your girlfriends and having a few drinks. The kind of drunk when you've lost complete control over your body and you're going to vomit.

The only difference was, I wasn't drunk.

"Katherine, can you get over here to us?" they called out.

There were red and blue flashing lights and cars all lined up close together in the street. I could see them kneeling down behind their cars. They were there — the people who came to help. But I felt completely alone.

What the hell, right?!? They were the ones with the bullet proof vests and guns and they couldn't come over to help me??

I could feel the life draining from my body. I could see the blood, pooling around me. I was lying in it. I felt so cold, I knew I was in trouble. My favorite pink Juicy Couture sweats stuck to me like paste to my body, which they later had to cut off and peel from my skin.

"No, I can't. Can someone help me?" I begged. For Christ's sake, help me!

My dad came out next with William in front of him.

"Sir, can you grab her and bring her over to us?" they called out again.

He bent down near me, grabbed my arm with a strength I never felt from him before. What the hell is going on? I was in shock — utter disbelief. My dad was bleeding profusely too.

"Come on, Katie, you gotta get up, we gotta go," my dad said. I had nothing left, but I had to get some strength and fast. With the table runner still wrapped around my hand, I lifted myself up to my feet with stamina that was not my own. We stumbled over to the caravan of cars as if we were in the school pick up line. Only we weren't kids, and they were in uniform.

We laid down behind the cars to wait for medical assistance to reach us.

She was there again. It was the second time we met that day. Only that time the officer was hovering over me. "I'm sorry, I'm sorry, I'm so, so sorry!" she repeatedly cried as if she had wronged someone who meant something to her.

With uninhibited, primal screams, like they were coming from someone else, someone who didn't have life draining out of her — I roared, "I FUCKING TOLD YOU! I FUCKING TOLD YOU HE WAS GOING TO DO THIS TO ME!"

Chapter 2
Happy Days

I was a single mom with Henry. He was my focus. I hadn't been on a vacation in years. When Tom asked me to go on a trip soon after we began dating, I was like, "Hell yeah!" We were looking online at all-inclusive resorts in Mexico and he booked one. He was scheduled to deploy to Iraq in November and we wanted to have a memorable trip together before he left.

Henry's dad agreed to watch him for the time I would be gone. Everything was working in our favor and I was so excited to have that time with him. I bought sexy new bathing suits and fun summer floral dresses for our trip in preparation for the fancy dinners. He brought his tailored suits and some island casual

Tommy Bahama clothes as well. He always dressed impeccably and looked very put together.

Then I got a phone call.

In the early morning hours of October 1, prior to our trip, Thomas was in a motorcycle accident. He broke multiple bones and our vacation plans immediately derailed. He was relieved of his deployment to Iraq due to his injuries. Tom called the resort and explained the situation and was able to push back our reservation to December.

I wasn't concerned about the vacation. I was just glad he was alive.

But once we did get to Mexico in December — oh yeah, I was into it. The resort was shiny and beautiful, perfection in paradise. Upon checking in, Tom leveraged his military influence and he talked his way to a room upgrade. He negotiated his way to one of the fanciest rooms at the resort. There was a sliding glass door that took up the entire front wall of the suite. Walking out onto the balcony led to a tropical feeling with bright green plants and trees in abundance on the grounds below. An intense, blue-water ocean filled the view beyond. It was posh.

I felt spoiled. I had never stayed anywhere like that before. To the right of the entrance to the room, there was a giant bathroom, with a floor to ceiling tiled shower. The room was expansive and open. It looked clean and bright — the pillows, sheets, and comforter on the king-sized bed, were crisp and white. It exceeded what I had imagined it would be.

We spent a lot of time in the sun near the giant pool. There were swim-up bars with all the drinks we wanted. It was the first and last time I sunbathed topless. I'd never exposed my breasts in public before, but I figured it was Mexico, I didn't know anyone anyway. It was an adventure I wanted to try. I felt comfortable with him. He was proud that I was game for going topless. I felt beautiful, sexy, and free to be me. I was having fun and getting away with the man who'd swept me off my feet. We slept in as long as we wanted. Our routine consisted of grabbing breakfast, going back up to the room to have sex, then down to the pool to have drinks, and back to the room for more sex and a nap. Wash, rinse, and repeat. It was fun, carefree, and exactly what I needed.

One afternoon, we went into Cancun to look around. Tom said I could pick out anything I wanted. He bought a lot of jewelry for me that day. I had been so focused on Henry, on having a child with me at all times, and so experiencing adult fun again meant a lot to me. Still, every day I called Henry to check in. I was grateful to work that out with his dad. I had a break from my role as a mom and I reignited the woman I wanted to be again.

It. felt. amazing.

The resort was all-inclusive, so we ate and drank often. One evening after drinks, we walked around to various gift shops in the lobby area and took silly photos of each other while trying on hats. I was being goofy, as was a normal behavior for me. Tom was not a let-loose kind of guy, though. To think of him doing that now, in retrospect, feels out of character for him. He did it though, he played along. He was mirroring me and my behavior, acting the same way I was.

Overall, we laughed a lot and had a good time together. Throughout the entire vacation, we filled many memory cards. That was before the iPhone, so we had a digital camera with us. We took tons of selfies or asked someone to take photos of us together. He acted proud to have me there with him and perhaps he was bragging with me on his arm — as if I was a prize that he had won. I felt lucky to be there with him. God, I thought he was so hot. We enjoyed our grown up time and got along well, with the exception of a couple, seemingly minor incidences.

We'd had some drinks at Señor Frogs and then went down to the beach. I was highly anticipating putting my feet in the sand and walking in the crystal blue water. Tom was still recovering from the leg fracture from the motorcycle accident, which required him to wear a protective boot. As I excitedly started heading out to the sand, he got pissy with me, protesting that he couldn't step on the sand with his boot. I said, "Well stay here. I'll just run down to the water and then I'll be right back." And that was what I did.

But get this: he followed me. Suddenly the boot wasn't a problem. I took a selfie of us together in the sand with the water behind us. I looked blissful. He was looking away from the camera, with a sneer on his face and a look I'd never seen before in his eyes — a low boiling anger. That picture always bothered me, gave me an uncomfortable feeling. I didn't delete it, I kept the photo anyway. Now, when I look at it, I'm reminded of the mood he was in by the expression on his face. I knew he was mad at me for going down to the water and not listening to him. You can see how I was in love with him, contrasted by the pissed-off look he had on his face.

There was another argument we had, in our room. I can't even remember what it was about. Usually our arguments were about nothing of consequence or importance.

What I do remember was his extreme behavior and how I felt.

During the altercation, he opened the sliding glass door to our balcony. With his injured leg and boot, he literally clamored over the balcony and walked along the ledge of the side of the building. I was terrified that he would fall. I began crying and begged him to come down and come back into the room. He eventually did, without remorse. The combination of his choice of action and his lack of sensing danger felt so extreme to me. It was very confusing. I couldn't quite put my finger on it at the time but it seemed as if he took pleasure in scaring me.

He took pictures of me the next morning, after waking up. My eyes were puffy from crying. I looked tired. And upset. I think he suggested make up sex. So I'd just get over it.

Chapter 3
Married: Day 1

I'm from Generation X. We were raised by the Baby Boomers. You know, so the messages we received were that, as young women — in addition to the lie that we could be and do anything we wanted to — we needed to find a man, get married, get a house, and have babies. So yeah, that was the "normal life" I sought. I married my college sweetheart, but divorced him by age 27. I didn't feel it was enough for me. Then I met and married Henry's dad. It was complicated. I'm not proud of how it started and we were likely doomed from the beginning. We did love each other, but there were challenges we just couldn't get past.

The best part of it, of course, was Henry.

So after the demise of my marriage with Henry's dad, I enjoyed the single life, but not for long. I knew I wanted something serious and lasting. And eventually a sibling for Henry. In my mind, everything was coming together with Tom. Finally, I was creating the life I wanted for Henry and me. It was my time and I felt I deserved it.

Tom and I had a whirlwind kind of romance. It clicked quickly, like a child learning to read. There was that moment when it felt expansive, it made sense, and I couldn't go back to the way it was before. I could only continue to move forward.

We hopped a plane to Vegas. We stayed on the Air Force base there. We booked a ceremony at a little chapel. I was three months pregnant with our baby. I felt complete, excited for the future ahead.

Then this happened.

The morning after our wedding, we decided to drive away from the Vegas Strip to have brunch. We had eggs benedict with hash browns and bacon. We had regular conversation. Then we got into the rental car and headed back.

In a casual and matter-of-fact way, Tom mentioned, "You know, when my ex left me, I went through the process in my head of how I would kill her."

You might ask if I felt chills, had a dramatic response upon hearing that, or wanted to jump out of the moving car. I did not. Because really, how do you process such a statement, delivered aloofly, as no big deal?

Think about it. It was the day after our wedding, we were driving back from brunch, and he delivered this random statement from left field. I wasn't expecting to hear such a confession from him. He didn't say it as a threat to me. It wasn't directed to me, or about me. It felt confusing. I wondered if he was joking. It was that nonchalant.

I looked at him. "What? Come on! You're not serious are you?" I said.

"Yeah, I was going to kidnap her, kill her, put her in the trunk, and dump her body," Tom said.

"That's not normal," I said. "What are you talking about?"

It was a very strange conversation. I didn't feel terrified. He displayed a lack of emotion when telling me his thoughts that, to me, conveyed a disbelief in my mind that he was capable of that type of criminal behavior. I certainly didn't believe he was capable of murder.

I continued saying that it didn't make sense to me. He went on to explain that the therapist he saw after his wife left him said that it was a normal part of the grieving process. That there may be some anger towards the other person and he might think about ways he would kill her. What he told me was that his therapist validated his thoughts as normal thoughts.

But I went right back at him. I told him I'd had relationships before and had been divorced before and I had never, ever, had a thought about killing someone.

He waved his hand dismissively and said, "Oh yes, well, it was just part of my process, but I got over it."

In retrospect, you're damn right. I should have jumped out of the car right then. At the time though, I didn't feel threatened. I couldn't relate to his thoughts, but I reasoned them into making sense in my head. Okay, sure, maybe some people do let their minds go there after a break up. But it was also a bizarre statement to bring up the day after getting married and I thought he couldn't really be serious. That was out of character for the man I married the day before.

I remember wondering if the therapist was right. Tom said she cheated on him — maybe he was hurt and angry. I was naive though. I didn't understand what he really was telling me. My mind could not comprehend that he was capable of murder.

It is only now that I can reflect back on that conversation and see it for what it was. Yes, it sure as hell was a direct threat towards me. He was telling me that he considered killing his wife before me because she had left him. Tom was telling me, the day after our wedding, that if I left him, he would kill me. It was a warning. It was a giant red flag.

I didn't recognize it.

Later that night, Tom began grilling me about past lovers and asking me direct and uncomfortable questions. This was under the guise of getting it all out on the table. He judged me for a one-night stand with a NASCAR driver. He was hammering me for details I didn't want to give. He grilled me on the entire scenario, wanting to know step by step how the tryst unfolded. Tom asked me to vividly describe my dating and sex life details, up until I met him.

I had an overwhelming feeling of discomfort. I should've told him to "fuck off." But I just kept answering his questions.

After demanding details of my past sex life, he began bragging to me about his conquests. And about how women were so attracted to him. Particularly, a married woman who worked with him at Andrews Airforce Base, a civilian woman who was frequently going into his office, flirting, laughing and touching his arm. I could feel jealousy bubbling inside as he described her as having long, blonde hair, which he loved.

I'd been there before. With men in the past. The processes of sharing details of your previous relationships as you get to know each other. But Tom was judging me. He shamed me, saying, "That's not very ladylike of you."

"Well, what about you?" I said. "You just said that when you were single, you had sex with a lot of different women."

"Well that's expected from men. It's not very ladylike of you," he retorted.

He was shaming me for things that were in my past, that I could not go back and change. It was acceptable, in his eyes, for him to do it because he had a double standard. Men can just sleep with as many women as they want, but a woman is a slut if she has sex when she's not married. I asked him about that and he just shrugged it off.

That was the day after our wedding.

Chapter 4
Fraud and
Corruption

When Tom was in high school, his father gave him an ultimatum. He could either enlist in the military or attend the University of Connecticut, but he'd have to live at home and commute. He opted out of the latter and right out of high school he enlisted in the Air Force and was stationed in Germany. As a soldier, he drove large trucks. He met a woman named Gianna, and became engaged and married at age 19. Eventually, they were stationed in North Dakota, and he was going through the ranks as a soldier.

A few years later, Tom left the Air Force, went to college and finished with a bachelor's and two master's degrees. He wasn't working while going to school full time and put his entire tuition on credit cards, while his wife kept them afloat financially.

Even though he was older than most, he commissioned to be an officer in the Air Force. At that time he was already 30 and most officers were just out of college. He was involved in government contracting. From what he told me, once he was commissioned as an officer, he left his wife of 10 years.

Shortly after he ended his marriage, Tom started dating Raquel, a single mother. She and her daughter moved with him from North Dakota to Wright-Patterson Air Force Base in Ohio when he was relocated. They cohabitated for a year and a half. He told me he kicked her out because she was lazy and never worked. He failed to tell me he had married her, but that's for later.

Tom loved to brag about his importance. He often bragged about how he bought bombs for the Predator, a remotely-piloted aircraft, when he was stationed at Wright-Patterson in the early to mid-2000s. He had top secret clearances and presented himself as a mission-critical person in the military. Tom told me all about when he was deployed to Saudi Arabia in 2000. He described it as a place where soldiers go to vacation during peacetime. Desert Storm was over and we hadn't moved into Afghanistan or Iraq at that time. It was a short, three-month, uneventful deployment where he claimed he met sheiks and was gifted expensive Persian rugs. He had them in his townhouse. He showed me stitching on the edge of two of the rugs — the maker's initials — which made them rare and expensive.

He did describe a couple of minor "incidents" he experienced in Saudi. He said he drove a Humvee into town with some other soldiers and they noticed some cars following them, trying to box them in. He said he had to move fast and get out of there quickly. He also described seeing and reporting what he thought might have been a bomb near a building by the base.

But that was the extent of the "excitement" in Saudi.

Melanie, his third wife, was stationed in his unit at Wright-Patterson. They met, moved in together after three months, and married quickly after that. I subsequently found out they too had a Mexico trip. They built a brand new house in Ohio, but shortly after they moved in, according to Tom, she had an opportunity in D.C. with her career, so they moved to Alexandria, Virginia.

I met Tom, according to him, six months after Melanie left him.

From the time I collided with him, I never saw Tom work a full day. If he put in three or four hours, that was a normal day for him. Usually he left his office on Andrews Air Force Base after lunch and would go home. He always had dinner ready when I came home from work. There was no accountability from his commander for the amount of time he put into his job. I never understood that.

I worked for a large insurance company and I occasionally worked from home. As a civilian worker I was accountable to my manager for my whereabouts and productivity. I couldn't leave for home in the middle of each day. I thought the military was rigid. That was until I noticed an officer could do whatever he wanted and get away with it. Tom showed me he wrote his own reviews. It wasn't his commander reviewing his work. It was Tom reviewing his own. He wrote stellar reviews about the amazing work he had done and the deals he sealed. To me, it appeared he did a whole lot of nothing. That work pattern continued through our entire relationship.

As we were planning to move from Virginia to Florida, where our house was being built, Tom used the back injury from his motorcycle accident to stay at home full time. He went to physical therapy but that wasn't considered working. He was not going into Andrews Air Force Base at all and was in touch with his command little to none.

He was never asked for reports on his treatment. The accountability was nonexistent. Tom said he put paperwork in to retire and it was taking time to process. He definitely never did apply for retirement from the Air Force. I learned that later.

I had the opportunity to take my job with me and I suggested I could to go to Florida with Will and Henry and Tom could stay behind to push for a finish on the paperwork. There was no way he was going to agree to that. He told me he could create a fake moving order to give to the movers. Then the military could pay our moving expenses. I asked what he was talking about.

He explained he had a scan of moving orders, it was just a PDF. He could changes dates, deployment location and hand the order to the moving company and they'd do it. I knew it wasn't legal but I couldn't stop him. There was no sense in arguing with him. I knew that's what he was going to do and it didn't matter what I said. He forged the paperwork. For whatever reason, I instinctively saved a copy of it on my computer.

In September 2010, the movers packed up the contents of our home in Fort Belvoir and it was off to Florida.

William and I flew down there while Tom took the auto train with Henry, who was pumped up for that experience. Essentially from the day we left Ft. Belvoir to January 2011, Tom was AWOL from the military. His commander, Colonel Travis Adams, had no idea his soldier was not in Virginia. He had no knowledge that Tom was living in Parkland, Florida. If Tom had a call with his commander, he made it sound like he was at home in pain and continuing with his physical therapy treatments.

He played the military. With zero qualms.

When people speak of Tom as honorable for serving in the military for 25 years, I feel irritated. Maybe worse than that. Irate. His military service was incomparable to the service other men and women in the military experienced. Tom checked out early on a daily basis and was AWOL for months. Others experienced the horrors of war, and put their lives on the line for us. Tom lied, pushed paper as a contractor for a few hours, and bought expensive oriental rugs.

And he committed fraud.

Nothing about that is honorable.

Chapter 5
The Marriage
Before Me

The history behind Tom and his wife before me was that she cheated on him. That was his claim anyway. He went on divulging details that she traveled a lot and was involved with a superior in the Air Force. The wife of the superior supposedly had contacted Tom and told him about the affair as well as told their commander. Tom brought in his commander along with her commander, and the next step was for her to face a court-martial. It is an admissible military procedure when a spouse cheats. Tom saved her career by de-escalating the court-martial process and withdrawing the grievance. They came to reconciliation and she sustained her career.

I saw Tom as the victim. He suffered. I hated that he had been treated that way. It tugged on my heartstrings. I also greatly admired that he was heroic enough to put aside his hurt and allow his ex-wife to continue with her career. Perhaps he was eliciting my sympathy, to have me on his side — intending for me to stand by my man who was treated so poorly. To feel scorn toward another woman for screwing him over.

But then there was blatant bragging from him about how he stalked her, his first wife. Wait, I mean his second wife. Or was it the third wife? He told me she was his first wife. I was an unevolved woman at the time. I was enthralled by him, I hung on to his every word. Not only his words but his circumstances and victimization too.

Tom was angry. When she left, she moved to a new apartment in Fairfax, the next town over from Alexandria. She didn't give him her address. She came back with police to retrieve her belongings. At the time, it was like, c'mon, really? She was making a big scene over that, how dramatic! He said he wasn't bothered about her taking her property but he was agitated that she was allowed to take a jewelry box full of jewelry he had bought for her. He didn't want her to have any of the expensive items.

I also received expensive jewelry as gifts from Tom.

He told the tale of the night when he drank a bottle of wine and popped an Ambien — he was trying to sleep and could not. In a drunken haze, he got on his motorcycle and drove from Alexandria to Fairfax. He had already found her undisclosed address at that point. He said he parked his bike, and scaled a six-foot wall in a gated apartment complex. He proceeded to break into her car in the parking lot and ripped out the sound system he had installed during their marriage. In addition, he let the air out of her tires.

He thought it was funny.

Tom told me he shared that story with others in his unit and they asked to hear it a couple more times because they thought it was so funny, too. He also said he had a CIA friend who installed a tracker on her car. Tom was able to log onto the computer and watch her comings and goings. His theory was that he planned to make a case against her that she was continuing to sleep with her superior. I asked if he had proved his case. He said he could never prove it because he couldn't get an exact identification of the superior when she was out and about.

Every time he was home, Tom said he would log on and watch where she was going. He also hacked her emails because he had

Keystroke installed on her computer and knew her passwords. He sent emails to people as though he was her.

There were no consequences for him. He got away with everything.

I discovered later that his ex never cheated on him. It was false. Clearly, she feared for her life and that's why she had police escort her to get her belongings. It was something that would become all too familiar to me.

Chapter 6
All About The Image

Blindingly white teeth, a big, perfect smile. Tom was very handsome when we met. I characterized him as "metro," but I didn't think a lot about it, other than I liked the fact that he took care of himself and knew how to dress and groom. Today, I can call a spade a spade. It was pure narcissistic vanity. He used his good looks to his advantage. I know he bewitched others on account of his presentation. Several times, I saw this working in action. He was a handsome, polite, friendly, white guy. He played it like a charm every time, and people did what he wanted them to do. He knew it and he used manipulation to get what he wanted.

Okay, but for real, he whitened his teeth obsessively. He enjoyed red wine and at least once a month he would whiten his teeth, saying wine had stained his teeth — which I never observed. Even then I thought it was bizarre.

We were newly dating and I invited him to go along with me to a friend's baby shower and he stopped to pick up a gift, a little girl's outfit. I was looking forward to introducing my new boyfriend to my friends. Sitting in lawn chairs, around a circle, everyone was chatting. A friend directed the question to Tom: "Where do you go to get your teeth done? They are so perfect and white." I found out later that after we left the shower, they were joking around asking what was up with that guy and his teeth, they were so white. It was just like in the episode of *Friends* when Ross leaves the teeth whitener on too long — an extra day — in preparation for his date. Tom's teeth were the same black light-glowing white.

Clearly, Tom was *very* conscious of his appearance and image.

Designer and name brand clothes and shoes were all he wore. He shopped all the time — like compulsively. His master bedroom closet was crammed full. In the guest room there was another closet chock full of more clothes, suits, ties, shoes, jackets, pants. I have never known a man who owned that much clothing. There was no way he could wear all the clothes he had.

He worked out, was a runner, and had a six-pack. There was an elliptical machine and weights in his basement. Working out was a daily routine for him. Tanning was also a frequent activity — he had a membership at a place in Alexandria. He felt that he looked healthier with a tan. I was influenced by that and I decided to tan too, to feel more attractive. And it didn't stop there.

He wanted me to be equivalent to him, with his status of appearance. He wanted me to be a reflection of him.

For example, Tom had moles on his face as a child and he showed me a picture of himself from middle school, pointing them out. They didn't seem very noticeable to me. He felt ashamed of them and had some removed as an adult.

I had many moles — they were in my genes. The mole on my nose became a signature to me when I was in my twenties during the 90s. Cindy Crawford and Paula Abdul were also known for the moles on their faces. It was a beauty mark of the time. When I lived in L.A., I considered acting and had professional headshots done. The photographer loved my mole, and he directed me in a profile shot to show the mole prominently.

Ever so slightly, Tom made a pivot — the move of a master chess player. He said my nose would look so much smoother if I had the mole removed. He said I would look prettier without it. When he looked at my face, he said all he could focus on was my mole. That was all I needed to hear. From that point on, I became ultra-self-conscious. What I thought was unique about me, something I liked about myself, became a culprit for him to find me unattractive. My self-worth existed in his hands. I craved his approval. I desired his acceptance.

I made an appointment with a dermatologist to have it removed along with two others on my left breast that Tom also had pointed out. Again, he said my skin would be much smoother without them. As they were removed, the area was numbed but I could still feel the pulling and tugging as the doctor was extracting the moles. Tears rolled down my face. I would have never considered removing my freaking moles without him suggesting it.

And get this. There is now a scar. My nose didn't heal correctly. The stitches opened and there was a deep, grooved wound that took a long time to heal. That was a decade ago and the scar is still there. Same with the ones on my breast. There are still small scars. The skin isn't smooth!

Fuck him. I wish I would have kept my moles — especially the one on my nose.

Tom also let it be known that he loved blondes, with medium length or longer hair. At the time we met, I fit that description. He would say things to imply that my hair had to stay that way, that he just loved my hair and I was such a "hot blonde." I had it in my head that if I ever changed my hair, he would no longer be attracted to me. In the past, I'd always experimented with hair color and lengths because I found it fun to change things up. But after he said that? No way was I changing it. I kept my hairstyle as he liked it.

In addition, I was becoming increasingly vigilant about my appearance, including my weight. William was a big baby — he weighed in at nine pounds. My pregnant stomach was enormous. After he was born, Tom would jiggle my stomach, my extra baby-belly skin. He would look at it with a slight sneer when I was undressed. I felt very uncomfortable about it, about his judgment of me. I did not like having extra fat either, even if it was because I just had a baby. Then he casually brought up the suggestion that I undergo a tummy tuck. I could have my post-baby stomach back and probably even better, he rationalized. I set up a consultation with a doctor and followed through with surgery. I was desperate to get it all hacked off. Will was only three months old. It was a major surgery. The recovery was long and horrendous.

I didn't care. I wanted to be his hot wife again. It was like being under a spell. It was hard to describe. It felt like desperation.

I can't reverse it now. What's done is done. Afterwards when thinking about it, I'd have a sick feeling over how much I changed my body for that guy, to feel his acceptance. I wish I wouldn't have been concerned with my stomach while having an infant. I didn't want to consider the long-term solution of dieting and exercising. I needed a quick fix. I *had* to stay attractive for him.

There is something deeply wrong and troubling about all of that. About misogyny and how girls are groomed from a young age through the messaging we get from society to have the perfect body, the perfect face, the perfect everything — so men will find us attractive. The "me" now would have told him to "fuck off," that I'm perfect the way I am. "If you don't like it then you can leave." But I wasn't that woman at that point in my life. I wasn't confident. I was highly insecure and my self-esteem was in the gutter.

Now, I want women to receive the message that they don't need to change their bodies to get acceptance from a man. If a man asks for that, he's a shallow piece of shit that doesn't deserve your time and energy.

Chapter 7
The First Date

When we met, I lived in a townhouse with Carolyn. She had twins, the same age as Henry. We thought we could have a bigger place, share expenses and help each other out. I wasn't dating much at that time. I had friends who were on Yahoo! Personals, similar to Match.com. They encouraged me to try it. What's the worst that could happen? Maybe a couple bad dates but at least I'd get a night out. I was skeptical of online dating. I definitely didn't think a serious relationship could evolve from it.

I was upfront in my profile description — I was a single mom with a 3-year-old son.

I was sitting at my computer and I decided to go through and wink at anyone I found attractive or thought I could be interested in. Thomas was one of the first profiles I noticed and winked at. I read his description and looked at his pictures and he was incredibly good looking. He was in superior shape, he didn't have kids, and I thought there was no way this guy was going to write back to me. He had a lot of vacation-type pictures on his profile. He was very tan, and was dressed in casual, nice-looking clothes. There were no military pictures. There was one of him smiling and leaning against a pool table.

Honestly, I thought he was hot as hell.

The next day, I logged in and discovered Tom had written to me. I was stunned — and pumped! We started talking a lot through our Yahoo! Personals accounts. We later exchanged emails and that's when he told me about his background in the Air Force. I thought, wow! This guy is also an officer? Swoon! I never dated anyone in the military. In my mind, when he disclosed that, I thought, he's serving our country, that's one of the most honorable things you can do. He had been serving for over 18 years and had top-secret clearances, for which he had to pass psychological evaluations. He told me he had worked on a lot of contracts for the Predator bomber. To me, it immediately secured his honorability and trustworthiness of character.

We went back and forth over five days or so. Then we started real-time messaging over Yahoo! Messenger. We flirted and got to know each other throughout the week. He asked me out on a date. I was giddy.

I made arrangements with Carolyn to watch Henry. Tom said he would pick me up. Normally, when I dated, I met at the determined location. I didn't let dates pick me up for safety reasons. I felt a trust with Tom, however. I guess good looks will do that — muddy your judgment.

When he arrived at my place, I opened the door and he had flowers. He said, "Hiiii, I'mmm Tommm," and he had this big, white, toothy smile. I know in my head I had a perplexed moment. *Something seemed off. Something about his inflection.* But I quickly brushed it away. He had flowers! I took them, put them in a vase and moved on. Looking back, I think there was a physical and mental reaction in my gut the moment I set eyes on him. It was easy to dismiss and I didn't dwell on it. I can still hear the way he introduced himself in my mind. That feeling in my gut was unsettling.

Tom had asked me if I liked sushi. I said I loved it. So he'd made reservations in Old Town Alexandria at a place called Kingfish. When we arrived, it was clear he had been there before. It seemed a lot of the wait staff knew him. I didn't think much of it, but it's probably where he brought a lot of his dates, including his ex-wife.

The sushi was good and so was the conversation. He was very attentive — looking right at me, like he was absorbing every word I said. I felt he was intrigued at what I was saying. The way he stared at me, it was as if there were hearts in his eyes. I thought he was the most handsome person that I'd been out with...ever. And I also felt I found someone very special.

We shared a couple of bottles of wine. He asked me if I wanted to see his place. I willingly said "yes" so we went back to his townhouse in Alexandria. It was a big, brick, beautiful house. The military gave him a stipend for off-base housing. We walked in and immediately I was impressed. Everything was in its place. The furniture was beautiful — like out of a showroom. He bragged about the rugs that sheiks gifted him when he was deployed in Saudi Arabia. Then he poured more wine and put the TV on to a romantic music channel. We started kissing, clothes started to come off and it progressed from there. I was excited this handsome, honorable man was interested in me.

God, I know it all sounds shallow. Like I was just into his looks. But it was more than that. I felt like he had the whole package. I felt like he was this top-quality guy.

Now I'm shaking my head at what I know.

Chapter 8
Growing Up

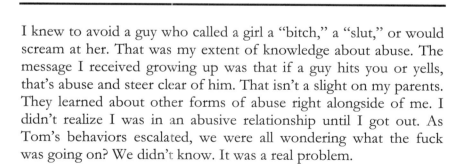

I knew to avoid a guy who called a girl a "bitch," a "slut," or would scream at her. That was my extent of knowledge about abuse. The message I received growing up was that if a guy hits you or yells, that's abuse and steer clear of him. That isn't a slight on my parents. They learned about other forms of abuse right alongside of me. I didn't realize I was in an abusive relationship until I got out. As Tom's behaviors escalated, we were all wondering what the fuck was going on? We didn't know. It was a real problem.

The Baby Boomer generation didn't really talk about the various forms of abuse. And if they didn't talk about it, or didn't know, there was no knowledge to pass on to their daughters or sons. My mother didn't grow up seeing abuse in her household. My father's father was an alcoholic, but there wasn't any domestic violence. I didn't grow up seeing abuse between my parents. I was in a complete naive bubble of privilege and it never occurred to me that I could experience abuse.

I was unprepared and lacked knowledge of coercive control, isolation tactics, emotional/psychological abuse, financial abuse — these things never crossed my mind at all. I wish I would have learned about these in middle and high school health classes. I wish they would have taught us about healthy relationships in high school in the 80s and 90s. But they didn't. I had a solid family and a comfortable upbringing. I didn't know I needed more. My parents didn't know I needed more.

So when my dad went with me to court to file a restraining order against Tom, that was new and terrifying territory. It just so happened that an organization in Broward County called Women in Distress had a permanent table set up inside the courthouse. Their booth had information on domestic violence, an abuse wheel, and pamphlets on the table for people to take. My dad picked up a pamphlet on emotional abuse and he read it. After we went home, my dad handed me the pamphlet and said, "Katie, read this. Just read it." I read it and there was a checklist with the signs of emotional abuse. I answered yes to every single sign of emotional abuse and there were ten items on the list. The skies opened. I thought, "Oh my God, this is abuse! I'm an abuse victim! I was in an abusive relationship and I didn't know it!"

I was 38-years-old. It was my third marriage. I'd gone through plenty of dating and boyfriends over two decades. But I never knew emotional abuse was abuse.

I started to go back through my dating history, beginning with my boyfriend in high school.

He used to knock my intelligence, called me a "blonde bimbo" and said that I wasn't very smart. He tried to tear me down. My next boyfriend was jealous, possessive and controlling. He chased me down the road one time because I was going to meet up with my girlfriends. He made me pull over and was screaming at me on the side of the road. I began to recognize more examples of men I dated who belittled me in some way, in an effort to make themselves feel better. Seeing that list changed my perspective about my entire relationship history.

We need to talk openly to young girls about the warning signs of abusive relationships. Throughout the school years, we need to talk about what is and isn't healthy in relationships. I should not have gotten to age 38 with zero tools on how to deal with abusive men.

Chapter 9
Body Shaming

At one point, during the first six months of dating, we were in the bathroom. I had showered, and he had just finished showering and was toweling off. I had a robe on which was open. Tom's eyes averted to my vagina. He wagged his finger toward me with a puzzled look and asked, "Has it always looked like that?"

My face and neck felt fiery as I was processing what he said. And I thought, "What does he mean? Why? What? This is MY vagina!"

"Yeah, this is how it's always looked. Why? Why do you ask?" I questioned.

"It just looks different than other women I've been with," he shot back.

I know I had a look of confusion on my bright red, now flaming hot face when I inquired, "What do you mean?"

Tom countered, "Their lips were smaller. Is it because you had a baby, like, did you get pulled down there?"

I didn't know. I knew my own body. I knew every woman's parts are different. But this was mine. It was what I'd known my whole life.

"No, this is how I've always looked," I shot back, feeling defensive.

"Well, I can tell that you've had a baby," he retaliated.

"What do you mean?" I demanded, trying to make sense of the shame I felt.

"Well, my ex didn't have a baby. I can tell that you have had a baby, plus Henry has a really big head," he concluded.

I quickly discontinued his line of questioning by making him aware I had never been told this by anyone else before. Tom explained that it was probably because they were too polite or didn't want to offend me if they didn't know me well. "But I know you and that's why I'm asking. Just curious," he said, "innocently." He proceeded this with, "Have you ever thought about labiaplasty? You can fix things down there after having a baby."

Then I started down the rabbit hole of wondering if men I'd been with before had thought this or were talking about me behind my back. Clearly Tom knew which buttons to push to undermine my confidence. With the moles, I could change, but not here, not with my private parts. And I certainly wasn't having labiaplasty.

That level of body shaming was horrifying. It was emotional warfare laced with a cocktail of, "but he loves me and still wants me." Maybe he is the only one who will love me like this. In one conversation, my self-esteem was crushed. My self-worth was in his hands. He was in control of it. He exposed my vulnerability as a mother and used it to create doubt in me. I feared if I was good enough for him. I feared that he wouldn't want to go down on me because he thought I was gross. And I feared he would meet a woman without a child and a different-looking vagina.

The tape recording of his words, what he said to me, continued to play through my mind for years after my marriage to Tom was over. When I started dating again, introducing intimacy in a relationship, I was filled with worry that he was judging my parts, like Tom did. It has taken a long time for me to let go of those words, and the intense feelings of shame. It took substantial time to move to feelings of acceptance of my body — a body that brought two human beings into the world.

Chapter 10
Big Or Small,
Lies Are Lies

He told lies throughout the entirety of our marriage. Tom would lie about things when he was trying to win me over. It was a falseness — a fraud, of who he was. When we started talking over Yahoo! Personals, his profile said he was 37. I was 34. He was within age range of what I was looking for. We began talking in early July. I thought he was 37 up until a week before his birthday, which was August 10th. He had to tell me that he was turning 40 on August 10, 2007 because we were going to L.A. to see his friends whom he met when stationed in Ohio. He knew, of course, they would say something about him turning 40.

We were messaging and he said, "I have to tell you something and I'm afraid you're going to break up with me. I put on the site that I'm 37 but I'm actually 39 and I'm going to turn 40 on August 10. I noticed that if I knocked off a couple years and put 37, the responses I got were more in my age range of what I was looking for than if I put 39. Being close to 40, I was getting older women and that wasn't my interest."

I asked why he didn't tell me that right away. He said he just forgot what was on his profile and then realized that I thought he was 37 and his birthday was coming up. "Please forgive me," he said. "I didn't mean to lie." I reiterated that he could have told me. The age difference wasn't an issue for me. I often thought back to that and wondered why he didn't say he was 39. I didn't get why he didn't mention it as we were getting to know each other. And I wonder how long he would have kept it up if there wasn't the big birthday coming up.

Tom knew I had two prior marriages, I told him that up front. I married my college sweetheart when I wasn't ready for marriage and it only lasted two years. My second marriage was to Henry's dad. Tom told me about his marriage to his ex before me, and called her his first wife. I was led to believe that she was the only other woman he married.

It was after our engagement when a mutual friend of ours, Jen, was over. Tom was in the hospital recovering from his motorcycle accident, and I'd come home one evening for a break. Jen and I were hanging out and chatting. She casually made a reference to a woman named Gianna, Tom's first wife. I said, "What?"

Jen's face looked bewildered as she realized I was oblivious of Gianna. She said, "Wait, you don't know about Gianna?"

"What are you talking about?"

"This is awkward," she said. "You'll have to talk to Tom about it, but he was married over 10 years to a woman named Gianna whom he met in Germany when he was young, about 19 or 20 after he enlisted. She was a German woman."

I was hearing that unexpectedly from a friend, not from Tom, as I was sitting on the couch with an engagement ring on and plans to get married. He had been married for more than a decade to a woman and I was oblivious! Why did he deceive me? He knew that I had been married twice. So why was it an issue if he had been married twice? Or three times?

We had a conversation on the phone. I called him after Jen left. I asked him about his marriage to Gianna. He told me that was not something he broadcasts. He said he found it difficult to overcome when he was dating because women were judging him for having more than one divorce. He said he didn't have kids with her, and they parted fine. End of story. He made it sound like it was classified and I didn't need to know about it. He had this ability to talk around it, to minimize it as if it was invalid.

Broadcast? He deliberately eliminated that fact. He *intentionally* left out a detail that encompassed a decade of his life. He didn't lie and tell me he was never married to Gianna. He lied by *never* informing me of her. He implied his first marriage of ten years wasn't important enough to remember. Soon, I would become well aware that I was not important to him either.

Chapter 11
The Gun Collection

My parents were educators as I was growing up. My mom taught third and fourth grade and was a reading specialist. My dad taught high school English, and then went into administration. We never had a gun in our home. If the parents of my friends had guns in their homes, I wasn't aware of it when visiting. I didn't grow up steeped in gun culture. My small town near Toms River, New Jersey, has since become more Republican and more of a gun place, but growing up as a little girl in the 70s and on through the 90s, guns were not on my radar. I never thought about them. I wasn't politically active but I did believe there was a need to control guns as in anything else dangerous. I never dated a man who owned guns until Tom.

Actually, Tom grew up near Red Bank, New Jersey, about an hour north of me. His dad was into hunting and they later moved to a compound in rural Connecticut. Tom showed me a photo of him at about 4-years-old, holding a dead duck with this blank stare on his face. It was an odd photo. In the spare bedroom, Tom had a showcase full of hunting rifles, about six, and most had been handed down to him from his dad. They were on display, like a collection of antiques. Then he showed me two massive, modern day shotguns. I never saw a gun like that before. He kept one under the bed, in case of an intruder — in "scary," deeply Democratic-leaning Alexandria, Virginia. There were at least two handguns.

I was intimidated by the guns. It was not normal to me to have a shotgun laying under the bed and handguns in drawers. At that point, I wasn't scared of him. I concluded that he was in the military, he knew how to shoot, and he'd been hunting with his dad since he was a kid. It was the culture he grew up in. In the military, guns are part of their job, at least part of their training.

When Henry and I moved in, I asked him to get safes and trigger locks for the weapons, especially for the shotgun under the bed. At first, he resisted. He said if someone broke in, he needed to be able to grab it and go. Henry was not a child who got into things and explored. He has Asperger's and at the time had a hyper focus on the thing he was interested in and that was it. I wasn't overly concerned about him finding the gun, although it didn't matter. I wasn't taking chances. Tom relented and ordered a safe for the handgun next to the bed and trigger locks for the rest of the guns.

Luckily we never had a crisis around this with Henry. Well, there was one time that Tom thought he heard a noise, got out of bed, naked, grabbed the shotgun and "swept the house." Like Rambo or something. I think he just wanted to create a dramatic scene for me. It was so awkward that he was going through the house with a shotgun and without clothes on. Henry was sleeping, so thankfully he didn't see it.

Needless to say, I am glad I insisted on gun safety.

And then, all of the sudden, Tom got on a kick about selling all the rifles. He had a falling out with his dad. He showed me the email. His father disowned him, called him a narcissist, and said he was divisive, manipulative, and that he wasn't a good person, and he really had nothing else to say to him. Tom was angry and wanted to sell all the hunting rifles his dad gave him. He figured out a way to get around the rules of selling firearms on *Craigslist,* as it was against policy. He would post pictures of the guns in the gun cabinet and say the gun cabinet was for sale — and other gun owners understood. It was like they had their own language.

He proceeded to sell all the rifles to private buyers. Obviously no background checks, nothing. I witnessed it myself but was clueless about gun sales and the need for background checks. Now, I realize how dangerous it was that he had no idea to whom he was selling these guns. Mostly overweight, white men would show up at our house, look at the rifles, give Tom cash, and away they went. He sold all the hunting rifles and one handgun. The handgun he sold to a young guy in D.C. They can't buy guns in D.C. but they can come over the line into Virginia, buy a gun and take it back into D.C. Tom was a part of that. He looked at the kid's license, which did nothing, and then sold him the gun.

Subsequently, there was a raid in this guy's brother's home and Tom's weapon was included in the stash. Since the serial number on the gun was traced back to Tom, ATF officials showed up at our home and asked Tom questions about the gun. Tom told them he did a private sale and I don't remember any questions about his process of selling the gun. Although there was an investigation over that gun and it was sold without a background check, no one seemed to care.

As our relationship progressed with time, we moved to a nearby Army base, Fort Belvoir. Tom got more guns when we arrived there although guns are not allowed on post in Fort Belvoir. They must be checked in and stored out of the home. Apparently the officers got away with it. Tom had all his guns in our bedroom and closet. The house next door had an arsenal, including AR-15s. No one ever checked.

Tom would take all of them out and line them up on the bed and clean them in front of me.

He knew I was uncomfortable with them. I already insisted on locks and safes. He would take them apart, clean them, and look at me. He took the handguns that had a laser on them and then play with the laser on the wall, as if it was a fun, Saturday afternoon activity. I would leave the room. We had a 5-year-old and a baby in the home. And at that point he had removed all the locks. I couldn't control that. I couldn't control him. There was no respect for my discomfort.

I was 500 times more likely to be hurt with the guns in the home. It never occurred to me to ever use a gun if I was in a situation and to turn it on him. That's not who I am. I lived in a home of intimidation — with an underlying feeling of discomfort and dread.

The irony? He would talk about wanting to teach William gun safety. He told Henry that you never point a gun at someone unless you intend to shoot them. He was all about educating the kids about proper usage of guns and being careful.

Then he shot us.

And now I'm a gun control activist.

Chapter 12
The Gaslighting
Begins

Tom had a "crotch rocket" when we met. A speed bike. Not like a Harley, where you cruise around and chill, enjoying the wind on your face. My uncle had a Harley and the previous summer I went on a long ride with him and I enjoyed it. I wasn't new to motorcycles. But I had never been on a crotch rocket before.

Tom told me stories when we were dating about how he would speed as fast as he could on the Capital Beltway, which was crowded with traffic. Not only was he putting his life in danger with this childish recklessness, he was endangering other lives as well. He was purposely reckless because he said his ex cheated on him, he was getting a divorce and he really didn't care anymore. He would speed in and out and around cars. He bragged about how he outran the police one time because they couldn't catch up to him. He got off on an exit and sped away.

On a weekend when Henry was with his dad, Tom invited me to go on a bike ride with him. I thought of it as an adventure but I did have some reservations about a speed bike. However, I was willing.

I trusted him.

He had to pick up something at his office on Andrews Air Force Base. So we took a ride from the townhouse in Alexandria over to Andrews, a straight shot down the Beltway. He kept the speed reasonable. I didn't feel scared or at risk. It wasn't too fast.

The second time, we took a ride at night and it felt different, maybe faster, but I thought it was because it was dark and there were a lot of cars around.

The third time I went on the motorcycle with him, it wasn't supposed to be a long ride. But he went for a good portion around the Beltway, far away from what we had planned. At one point he was speeding so fast I felt like I was going to fly off the back of the motorcycle. I was holding on to him around the waist for dear life, hugging as hard as I could. I couldn't crouch down like him so I was getting the full brunt of the wind. I had tears streaming down my face. I was terrified and was thinking, "Just hold on, you're not going to fall off. Keep holding on Kate." I couldn't tap him to slow down. I was paralyzed because I had to hold on for my life.

I envisioned myself flying off the back. I envisioned Henry.

When we got back, I took the helmet off and he saw my tears. "That was scary and too fast, I said. "I'm not going on the bike again."

 "Oh you're overreacting, I had control of it."

I came back with, "No, you don't understand. You were operating it and you were in the front, and I felt like I was going to fly off the back of it."

"You're being dramatic and overreacting. That wasn't going to happen," he replied.

"If you would have hit a bump and I lost my grip, I would have flown backwards and died."

He shrugged it off. He knew I was scared when he drove 125+ mph on the Beltway, swerving around cars. But he showed no empathy or concern for my safety. Instead he put the blame on me as if I was overreacting.

I began to feel my fear was unjust. He insisted he had control of the bike and I was being dramatic. I began to feel ridiculous. Later when I would have a random flashback or thought of that ride, I physically shuddered. All the "what ifs." I really was lucky he didn't hit a bump or lose control over the bike because I would have died. He never apologized for his reckless behavior.

Or maybe he never considered his behavior to be reckless. Or maybe he got off on making me feel afraid.

Probably that.

Chapter 13
My Pregnancy
With William

When we went to Mexico, I had been on birth control pills for a long time. I am unsure whether he messed with my pills or if my inconsistency in taking them at the same time each day was the factor. It wouldn't have surprised me if he had messed with my pills. Either way, I became pregnant with William in December, 2007.

The initial look on his face was dark and blank when I told him of my pregnancy. We were already engaged and planned to get married in the summer of 2008. We already made plans for our future. I jumped on him and hugged him and he hugged me back but there was still a lack of connection. I wrote it off that he was probably in shock. He was married twice before without kids and it was new to him. I, on the other hand, was excited. We would be a family. I was ready for another baby and to give Henry a sibling. I was 35. My pregnancies with William and Henry were similar. I had morning sickness in the first trimester and the second and third trimesters were "normal."

But there was a big difference during my pregnancy with William

It was considered a healthy pregnancy, at least for the baby, but I felt quite sick and unstable throughout. I experienced severe daily panic attacks where I was hospitalized at least two or three times. I thought I was dying and the ambulance would come to our house. One time was so bad, my hands became almost paralyzed, like claws, and I couldn't breathe. I now wonder if he had been giving me medication, or lacing my drinks or food. It was odd and unsettling. Every time they would check us, William was fine but my blood pressure would go through the roof and they would keep me overnight to monitor me. They could never find anything.

Tom went with me to all of my OB appointments on Andrews Air Force Base. One time in particular, after I had met with the doctor several times over that general fear of discomfort and panic, the doctor came out into the waiting area and told Tom he was just going to talk with me. Tom seemed indifferent. This was the only doctor who had ever asked me this, a male, military doctor. He said, "You are having these recurrent problems Kate, is everything ok at home? Is he doing anything to you? Are you safe?"

I thought those were the most bizarre questions. I had no idea I was in the middle of an emotionally, psychologically abusive relationship. I remember looking at him like he had three heads. "No, everything is fine, I've never been happier. I don't know what's going on with me or why these things are happening, but it has nothing to do with him." But in reality, it had *everything* to do with him. There was something inside me that knew how I was feeling was wrong, yet completely pushed out any inkling that maybe something nefarious really was going on.

I was in absolute denial. Deep denial.

There was a moment when a doctor suspected something was wrong and cared enough to ask. There was nothing he could do though, if I said everything was fine. I understood that. The problem was that I didn't know. I didn't know what emotional abuse was. I didn't even know anything was wrong with my marriage — with his behavior.

Maybe if the doctor had asked a different question. "Is he isolating you in any way?" If he had given me examples rather than a general question, maybe I would have recognized it. There has to be a way to ask the questions differently.

I had an induction scheduled for September 22, 2008. William's birth was on Andrews Air Force Base. My parents came and helped with Henry. We drove from Fort Belvoir to Andrews that morning. I was nervous and excited at the same time. We knew he was a boy and already named him William. Tom seemed excited too. He was present and supportive. He stayed with me the whole time. When you're induced, it can be boring and we just hung out together. William was my second baby, so his birth was much easier than Henry's. I had an epidural; I pushed a few times and out came William.

But Tom's behavior right after the birth was so...awkward.

He was doing this weird shaking all over, almost convulsing type of thing. It was as if he was forcing himself to feel something. He was forcibly shaking his whole body.

I looked at him quizzically and asked if he was ok. He answered that he was just so overwhelmed. It was dramatic. And seemed forced.

That's because it was. It was a totally fabricated and inappropriate reaction. Because really, the man feels nothing.

Chapter 14
Henry In The Middle

Henry's dad and I had established a successful co-parenting relationship for three years after our divorce. We got to a point where we'd have dinner together, the three of us, at a diner. We wanted to show Henry that we could be friendly and raise him as a team, without being married. We were in a good place.

Very quickly after meeting Tom, however, that changed. He sized up Henry's dad. He saw we were civil and working well together. It became Tom's mission to drive a wedge between us.

He hovered around when I was on the phone with my ex. The discussions were always about Henry. Yet, Tom stayed within hearing range and when I got off the phone, he would tell me I was too friendly and my ex would probably get the wrong idea. He would question me, asking if I still had lingering feelings or love for my ex. I couldn't convince him enough that the answer was no. Tom began chipping away, saying that I needed to dial it back with the friendliness and I needed to make it more like a business transaction. He claimed his therapist had told him that is the way divorced couples should behave, business-like, especially when one or both of them is establishing a new relationship. It was about building trust with Tom and by having a business-only relationship with my ex, I could convince Tom I was trustworthy.

In the beginning, if I received an email from Henry's dad, I would occasionally show Tom. Sometimes I wanted his input for a particular response. It quickly developed into Tom requiring me to blind copy him on every email I sent so he could edit the response. Tom would always make changes, make it more business-like. He would point out where I was giving in too much. He would change the entire tone of the email, to the point where it didn't even sound like me.

I knew how to co-parent with my ex. And, I had figured out the best way to communicate with him. Tom changed it, not only by coming across business-like, but he changed the tone to a snappy one. I knew that my ex wouldn't react well to that, but I didn't push back. If I did, I'd get accused of still being in love with him. I didn't want to deal with that.

It changed the entire dynamic. And not for the better.

Tom also completely put his foot down on any activities between the three of us. It was a devastating blow to the co-parenting relationship between my ex and me.

In addition, Tom was slow to warm up to Henry. He only seemed to tolerate him. I wrote it off as I wasn't looking for a replacement dad for Henry — he had a dad, we had it covered. But what he did do was swoop in and buy him things. He would take us to the BX on Andrews to get new clothes. It was higher end, for a BX. He bought Henry a bike and a Nintendo DS. Tom looked like a good guy.

But he would call Henry "his dad's son" and in the next breath, he would say that Henry's dad was a "retard." He did this often and always in front of Henry.

"You cannot disparage his dad, do not say that," I said. "He is Henry's dad and that is inappropriate."

Then Tom would turn it on me, by accusing me that I must be having feelings for my ex — why else would I be defending him? It would lead to an hour of attempted convincing that I no longer had feelings for my ex.

None of it mattered. It continued anyway.

Tom also resisted the sleeping arrangement Henry and I had. When I was single, living in the townhouse, Henry's bedroom was down the hall from mine. I left my bedroom door open in case Henry had trouble sleeping, going to sleep and staying asleep, or had an accident. I had always done that. He was between 3 and 4 years old — before he was diagnosed on the autism spectrum at age 5.

When we moved in with Tom, he had an idiosyncrasy that he had to sleep in a room with the temperature of a meat locker. He had installed an air conditioning unit in his bedroom. He insisted the door remain closed. The unit was so loud, it didn't feel safe to me to not be able to hear Henry. I went through all the what ifs as a mom: what if someone breaks in and takes him, what if I don't hear him when he wakes up. I felt vulnerable. I didn't like the door to be closed. Tom said there was no way he was sleeping with it open. His compromise was to buy a baby monitor and put it next to our bed, but with the volume off. So I could see Henry but not hear him.

My sleep was interrupted most nights because I would wake up, look at the camera and make sure he wasn't agitated or up and moving around. Henry coming into our bed during the night was no longer an option. Not even coming in on my side to lay by me. If I needed to get up and go into his room I could do so. And I did on a couple of occasions. Tom was pushing me past my motherly instincts.

It had to be his way at *all* times.

Other ordinary things about Henry irritated Tom. When Henry was potty training, learning to pee standing up in front of the toilet, there happened to be drops of urine on the rim of the toilet seat. It was not something I noticed, since I didn't and still don't lift the seat to pee. It was a Saturday morning and Henry and I were in the basement of the townhouse watching TV, when Tom came down with this dark, cloudy, pissy look on his face.

"What's the matter?" I asked.

"He's peeing on the seat," Tom said.

"Ok," I said, "Well, wipe it off."

"He shouldn't be doing it," he said. "He should wipe it off."

"He's 3 years old," I responded.

He came back with, "Then you should wipe it off."

"I didn't even think of that as something to pay attention to. I don't pee like a boy."

His mask was still on. This was early in our relationship and I think he realized that he was behaving harshly. He recovered quickly.

"Oh right, I didn't even think of that. How would you know?" he said. "Well yeah, he's going to have to wipe up after himself."

So I taught Henry how to do that. He didn't always remember but when he didn't, I sure as hell did because I didn't want it to be an issue.

Chapter 15
Guy Friends?
Forget It!

When I met Tom in July 2007, many of my friends were exiting MySpace and getting onto Facebook. I had a lot of friends and family opening accounts. I let Tom know I was going to join and immediately a dark gloom washed over his face. He went on to tell me that it was not a good idea. He claimed his therapist said those sites were bad for relationships because people were reconnecting with their pasts — people they used to date and their high school crushes. "It's about trust," he said. He had been cheated on before, after all, and it would be a constant source of worry for him. It didn't matter how much I reassured him that I loved him, that I was committed and I wasn't going to cheat. Nevertheless, Tom dug his heels in, said it wasn't a good idea and he believed his therapist. I complied. Was Facebook really worth having difficulties in my relationship? Most of the people I wanted to be in touch with, I could call or email anyway, I rationalized.

But then with time, I really wanted to get on. I wanted to connect with my friends and see what they were up to. It had nothing to do with men and sex, like he implied. So I came up with a compromise. I told him I felt very strongly about signing up, that even my parents were on Facebook. I would join and only have female friends. Any men on my friends' list would be family members or spouses of friends.

He didn't like it but he agreed to it. He also imposed another caveat. If I ever got a friend request from a man who was not a family member, I would need to tell him, or the trust factor would be broken. I complied at first. "Oh so and so from high school friend requested me and I denied it," always escalated into "See??? They all want to fuck you. This is why I have such a problem with Facebook. It's not that I don't trust you, I don't trust them."

"You understand that it's a two-way street, right?" I'd say. "Like, I also have to show interest. So who cares if they have visions of wanting to fuck me? I can't control that. I can control myself and I'm not interested in anyone else."

I felt like a broken record.

I probably told him about male friend requests three more times before I realized it was easier not to tell him. It was stupid — we'd have the same go around. It was incredibly frustrating and annoying. Every so often he would ask if I had a friend request from a guy and I'd say no, I had my core friends list, so I was not being asked.

I did turn other men down when they would friend request me. I did what I said I would do. He would ramp up every so often and get angry with me about Facebook. It occurred in cycles. I even gave him my password at that point and said, "Go look; I have nothing to hide from you." In fact, I put the password on a Post-it note and stuck it on the computer screen. If he did look, he didn't admit it to me. It was an unnecessary jealousy and possessiveness over nothing. He wanted to control who I was interacting with on social media. But it's hard to keep someone under that kind of extreme control when it comes to social media.

He would read my emails early on, too. One time, I was in the bathroom bathing Henry and heard Tom say, "Who the fuck is

Alex?" I could feel my face get hot and I realized he was looking at my emails.

I had a platonic lunch with a guy I used to work with whose office was across the street from mine. It was within the first week I was dating Tom. "Why didn't you tell me?" he demanded. I said it wasn't anything I thought was a big deal, that it was nothing, that we'd been friends for many years. He ordered me not to email him again. I maintained my stance that it was harmless and that he had no right to go through my email. I knew once my face became red hot, he was somehow going to twist it and make it my fault.

His entire basis for jealousy was that every man wanted to fuck me. It was like, don't make eye contact, don't talk to anyone, or Tom will strike a jealous rampage. He completely dismissed the fact that I would have to be a willing participant in all of that, and it wasn't anything I was interested in.

The jealousy and possessiveness was not attractive — nor was it fun. It was stressful. I now realize jealousy is not cute, as in, "Oh he must love me so much, he just doesn't want to share me." No. The reality is it's about having power and control. Feeling a sense of ownership, and other men feel threatened by that. Throw in a piece of insecurity, too. It's extremely damaging. It goes back to toxic masculinity and he definitely reflected that. I never knew when something benign could piss him off.

After we broke up, I started friending *everyone* on Facebook.

Chapter 16
Isolation 101

It was gradual. The isolation. I was living with Carolyn when I met Tom. She and I had signed a one-year lease and when I moved in with Tom part way through the year, I continued to pay my portion of the rent so she would be covered. She was also a single mom, I made an agreement with her and I wanted to follow through.

Every chance he got he would make little digs at Carolyn for taking my money. I explained I had signed a lease and I needed to pay it. Our agreement was that I had paid more rent as I made more money than she did, so I had the master bedroom and Henry had his own room. Carolyn took the whole basement with her kids and we shared the kitchen and living area.

I found out after I moved out that Carolyn had moved into the master and Tom said that it was not right that she did that. He was chipping away at my friendship with her, pitting me against her. And it worked. I felt annoyed. But then again, why would she stay in the basement when no one was living in the upstairs? He also showed no interest in getting to know her at all. Henry and I saw less and less of her as I spent more time with Tom. Henry and I would go and visit her once in a while at the townhouse. Eventually our friendship fell by the wayside. That was the first relationship he targeted.

The second was Henry's dad. He made it his mission to drive a wedge between me, my ex and our co-parenting relationship. The other part of that was that I once had a close relationship with Henry's older sisters. I met them when they were 3 and 5 years old. At the time we split up, they were 7 and 9. Their mom would let me see them sometimes and I would pick them up from school and take them to dinner. They stayed at my apartment a few times. The minute Tom heard about that, he said, "No, you *were* their stepmom. And you're *not* any longer. It's not appropriate for you to see them anymore. That's detrimental to our relationship. You're stuck in the past, it's unhealthy for them, and it's time to move on. You have a new relationship."

I said well, they're Henry's sisters and I would like to maintain some kind of relationship. But there was absolutely no way he was letting that continue. He hung our relationship over my head. I slowly stopped seeing them.

I was so influenced by him, eager to be accepted by him and please him that I went along with the things that he said.

It was pathetic. And wrong.

He took aim at more of my relationships. My dear friend Natasha lived in D.C. and I'd known her for almost 20 years. She'd always been a good friend. She always had my back. It was her baby shower that Tom and I went to, when everyone noticed his iridescent teeth. I started seeing less and less of her, too.

Tom went with me to see her baby in the hospital. During my pregnancy, we went to see her one time in D.C and had lunch. But after I had Will and we moved to Fort Belvoir, I barely saw her. When I did, she would always come to Fort Belvoir. I never went to D.C. When she visited, he would make himself scarce, go upstairs after a while and text me, badgering me. I recall one specific time. It was summer and we had a big inflatable pool behind our house. Natasha's daughter and William were splashing in the pool — she and I were sitting in the sun, hanging out. He started texting me. I could tell by her face she thought it was weird and was getting annoyed that I couldn't give my full attention to her since I was having to respond to his texts. His texts were stupid. They were nothing important. But there was this underlying understanding that I needed to respond to them or there was going to be a problem when she left.

At one point he came out wearing his robe and he was naked underneath it. The interaction was uncomfortable for me, while having my friend over. He created it to be that way.

I would say that the height of my isolation was at Fort Belvoir. We were living on a military base where everyone had to have ID to get onto the base. The base had everything so it was not really necessary to leave it.

And, even as I started making friends with the military wives and joined their Bunko games, he'd text me the entire time. There was zero reason he'd need my attention. If there was anyone he should have trusted it was the military wives. It was stressful. I never felt I could put my phone away and just have fun with the girls. He was always demanding my attention. It was all about him at all times and anything that took attention away from him was a threat. Even the military wives at Fort Belvoir.

Before Tom, I was a very social person. I loved to talk with people and get to know them. I was super friendly. I went to parties. I was invited to everything. My relationship with Tom was traumatic and it took a toll on me.

Once we got to Florida, things began to unravel quickly. Within the first three months, he began to chip away at my brother and sister-in-law. He'd say he didn't like my sister-in-law — claiming she was jealous and threatened by me. He said my brother would never stand up for me. Had things gone a different course, had I stayed and not left, he would have gone after my entire family. But he never got that far.

Chapter 17
And The Attention
Goes To...

I struggle to find happy memories with Thomas. My memories are tainted. They don't seem real. Our relationship was a fraud.

I was most enamored with him, googly-eyed if you will, before the control and manipulation was deep set, or at least before I was aware of it.

Our relationship was fairly new when my childhood best friend was having a party in Atlanta in celebration of her 30th birthday. It fell on a weekend when Henry was with his dad and I planned to go. I wanted to bring Tom with me to meet my friend and her parents who were best friends with my parents. Her mom was one of my favorite people, someone I trusted and could talk to while growing up. Tom and I booked the tickets to Atlanta and we stayed with Heather and her husband.

It was my hope that Tom would spend time with Aunt Donna, who was always so much fun to be around, and Uncle Greg, who was an Army veteran and served in Vietnam. He had a proud military history. I thought they would have a lot in common. Heather's husband Dan was very easy-going. Heather was super funny and we always had the best laughs. I thought Tom would enjoy being around them.

He didn't. He wasn't engaged at all.

He spent far too much time on their computer, which was upstairs and away from everyone else. He didn't interact with the men. If he was downstairs, he'd sit with me as I talked and laughed and carried on with Aunt Donna and Heather. I was so excited for him to meet the family that was so close with mine. But he didn't interact much at all. At one point I found him at the computer again, and he mentioned he was going through his old Yahoo emails. He found a bunch from his ex and was telling me details.

It was an attempt to pull my attention back to him. An attempt to make me jealous.

I asked if he was deleting the emails. He explained it was so interesting to read the back and forth banter between them. It was bizarre and creepy. And I didn't want to make an issue of it. I was with the family I cared deeply about and I was going to enjoy it.

I left him at the computer and went back downstairs.

Dinner for Heather's 30th party was in downtown Atlanta. We had a good time and took lots of pictures. I felt proud to be with him. I felt like we complemented each other. We looked good together. I thought I had a great catch and it was my opportunity to show him off. I knew Uncle Greg would feel that Tom was an outstanding guy. He was military and active duty, after all.

It's interesting when looking back at the pictures from our relationship. When we were at the bar on Heather's birthday party night, my expression showed I was over the moon. I had a genuine smile, a genuine sparkle in my eyes. I wanted people in my life who were important to me to meet him and like him. I was happy.

But thinking back, I didn't receive any feedback after we left. No one complained about him. But no one had any positive comments at all.

My guess is he came off as arrogant and aloof, so they just said nothing. Often that silence speaks volumes.

Chapter 18
Acceptance Didn't
Exist

We got through the first year of dating without drama during birthdays and holidays. For the most part, that year was "normal." The following year, 2008, William was born in September. We had Henry's 5th birthday party in Fort Belvoir, in the officer's community club house. William was one month old and I was feeling stressed out. There were a ton of people there, including the military wives, and all of their kids.

My friend Natasha brought her daughter, Tiffany, to the party. She told me later how all the kids were running around the clubhouse and Tiffany, then a toddler, was playing nearby. Henry ran by Tiff and accidentally knocked her over. Natasha helped her daughter up and knew that Henry meant no harm. However, Tom just laid into Henry and accused him of being stupid and careless. Henry was sorry and Natasha told him not to worry to continue his play, but Tom wouldn't let it go.

He had to find fault in Henry.

For my birthday that year, Tom bought me a professional grade Canon camera and lens. I loved taking pictures, and was getting good at it. I had a good eye. On Christmas Eve, our tree was up and I was getting the boys ready for bed. I decided to capture a Christmas Eve photo of the boys before they went to bed. I sat Henry cross-legged in front of the tree and I placed William in Henry's arms. I ran into the other room to grab my camera, when all of a sudden I heard crying and yelling. I ran back into the living room to find Tom yelling and pointing at Henry, who was crying. William was on the carpeted floor, on his back, crying too. I scooped up Will and Tom screamed that Henry dropped him. "He fucking dropped him!!" he yelled.

I knew that Will was ok. They were on a carpeted floor. I picked him up and checked his head just to be sure. I could see nothing was wrong. I then turned to comfort Henry, to tell him it was okay, that it was an accident.

Tom immediately began to lay into me. "He's going to fucking kill that baby! He did it on fucking purpose! He dropped him on purpose!"

What really happened was William spit up on Henry and when Henry lifted his arms — Will rolled off his lap onto the carpet. That was the extent of it. Tom turned it into a big, dramatic event. Henry continued saying, "I'm sorry Tom, I'm sorry Tom," as he was crying and gasping for air. I assured Henry that it was an accident. Tom suddenly grabbed Will from my arms and took him into the guest bathroom nearby and turned on the light. He dramatically examined Will's head as I went in and repeated that Will was fine. He said "It's not fine! SEE?? Look!" and pointed to his head. There was nothing there.

I took Will back from Tom, gathered Henry, and went into the family room to sit on the couch and try to calm them both down. It was a lot all at once. The next thing I knew, asshole walked over, grabbed both of my wrists with one of his hands and took William out of my arms with his free hand. He said, "I'm leaving here. I'm going to the barracks."

It was Christmas Eve.

I looked at Henry. Tom turned and walked down the hallway. I went after him and grabbed a hold of the collar of his t-shirt and pulled. "Please don't leave! Give me the baby, don't leave." I knew. I sensed danger and I took Will out of Tom's arms. I grabbed Henry and ran with both kids upstairs, into Henry's room, slammed the door and locked it.

In my haste, I forgot there were small keys above the molding of each door. I heard him grab the key and unlock the door. He walked in with that smug look on his face.

"Yeah, well, I called the MPs and they're coming. They're going to arrest you and you're going to jail tonight." He proceeded to show me where I had pulled the collar on his shirt to get him to stop from leaving with Will. There was a mark.

I didn't believe then that I pulled hard enough on his collar to leave an impression. I still don't believe it.

I believe he gave himself the mark.

He'd taken a digital picture of the mark on his neck and showed it to me. "I have the evidence here in the picture, you're going to jail tonight."

He said it in front of Henry. Henry began hysterically crying and then I was too. I begged him to call off the MPs. It was Christmas Eve. It was a misunderstanding. "Can we just forget about it??"

He let me hang in fear for a long time. They never came. Now I'm sure he never called them in the first place. I was terrified I was going to get arrested in front of my children on Christmas Eve. It was horrendous. I just wanted to calm Henry down, to get him into bed, so he could anticipate waiting for Santa, like kids are supposed to do on Christmas Eve.

I don't even remember much of what happened the rest of the night. It was traumatic. I blocked it from my memory. My behavior at that point in our relationship was to be good, to behave. I didn't push back at him. I pretended that nothing had ever happened. I know I put all the presents under the tree later that night. Then, the next morning, we had the shiny, happy, picture-taking Christmas morning like every other family.

Except in all the pictures you could tell I had been crying.

When I cry a lot, my eyes get very puffy. I was sad. I was trying very hard to make a normal, happy Christmas for the kids. The trauma from the night before lingered on my face. I didn't tell anyone about that night. That was when the shameful feelings began. It wasn't a happy occasion, other than seeing Henry smiling and excited about his presents, and also because it was Will's first Christmas.

Then came New Year's Eve.

The first New Year's Tom and I were together, we knew I was pregnant. It wasn't planned, it was random, but we had sex on that night. It happened that as the clock struck midnight — we were in the middle of things. We joked that we were "banging" in the New Year, having sex from 2007 to 2008.

New Year's had always been filled with tradition in my family. When we were growing up, we would always stay up until midnight and then we would run outside and bang pots and pans in the front yard and yell, "Happy New Year!" It was a tradition I wanted to follow with my kids. That year, 2008, when Henry was five, I said if he could make it up until midnight, I wanted to bang pots and pans with him.

That was something Tom knew I wanted to do.

Henry was still awake at 11:45pm on New Year's Eve 2008, and all of the sudden, Tom was demanding me to go upstairs and have sex with him. He said he wanted to do the same thing we did together the year before. He wanted us to be having sex during the countdown and into the New Year. I had been pumping up Henry about staying up and banging pots and pans together and I reminded him Henry was excited. We would bang the pots and pans and I would put him to bed and then we could do it.

That wasn't enough for him.

He got red in the face, he was pissed off, and he went storming upstairs and began texting me. I stayed downstairs with Henry — I was holding my ground on my tradition with Henry as I promised him. Tom was blaming me and shaming me through his texts — giving me a bunch of shit that I was a bad wife. He said it was supposed to be our tradition. Sex into the New Year was our new tradition. He accused me of choosing Henry over him. "He's a child," I said, "and you knew I had planned this." He said Henry didn't know if it was midnight or not and I could have already done the pots and pans. I said we are watching the ball drop on TV.

I didn't give in. Well, I did a little bit.

I took Henry into the guest room and we quietly banged pots and pans. We didn't go outside in the yard like I wanted to do. I didn't want to upset Tom any further. Now it fucking pisses me off. I can picture Henry and me in the guest room going ding, ding, ding, not to make Tom any more mad.

Fuck him.

I put Henry to bed afterwards and went into our room. Tom gave me the cold shoulder. He ignored me. I didn't do it his way. We didn't have sex. I cried myself to sleep. Repeat — the puffy eyes on New Year's Day. I was walking on eggshells. It was hell. I never knew what he was going to accuse me of and how I was going to piss him off.

His tumultuous behaviors seemed to be increasing. Every event was dramatic, including every family event.

When we were in Florida in 2010, he got pissed off at me on my birthday. He left and rode his bike back home to our house and blew up my phone with text after text. Then he ignored me when I got home. At Christmas, he was outside with Henry and his new fishing pole. The fishing line got tangled. Tom laid into Henry about untangling the line. Henry came in crying. Wanting to smooth everything over in front of my family, I deflected and suggested we open gifts. Tom came inside, saw the kids opening presents and became visibly angry. He blamed me for not waiting for him and took off, then blew up my phone again.

On New Year's 2010 -2011, he was pain-pilled out of his mind. Our neighbors were having a pig roast and invited us over. My parents were over and Will was little. I went back and forth a couple times from the neighbor's to our house. Tom was a train wreck. He was going back and forth constantly agitated. He wouldn't sit down. He'd go to the neighbor's, do a bunch of shots, then come home upset, leave and do it all over again.

Around midnight, the fireworks in Parkland began going off. He pulled me aside and was acting so strange, so wired.

Then he told me he just shot his gun.

I was like, "What? What do you mean you just shot your gun?" He said when the fireworks were going off, no one could even tell that it was gunfire. I demanded to know where he was doing that. "I was shooting at lizards between the houses," he said. It was pitch dark outside, it made no sense to me at all.

"There are children next door! What were you thinking?" He just laughed. He thought it was hilarious he shot his gun in the neighborhood between homes — where families live.

Let that sink in. This psychopath shot a gun in our new neighborhood.

He was a piece of shit.

Chapter 19
Power, Control &
Domination

My beloved grandfather, "Papa" as we called him, was quite a character. He had a big personality, always laughing and smiling. Everyone loved him. He and my grandmother lived in a small town, Pepperell, MA. He was the town veterinarian, caring for both farm and domesticated animals. He was adored by everyone who knew him, no exaggeration.

In 2008, he took a fall in their home and his health began to decline. My grandmother suffered from dementia, so they went together into assisted living. Over the next year and one-half, his body began to fail him and in August of 2010, he passed away. It hit our family very hard. We were emotional and came together for his funeral and to celebrate his life. I flew up by myself while Tom stayed behind with baby William. I chose to go alone because Tom demanded so much of my attention, and Will was little. I knew I wouldn't be able to focus on my family. It was a good call, especially to be there for my mom. All of us cousins were able to get together with cocktails and tell Papa stories. We cried and laughed. It was truly a special bonding time with my aunts, uncles and extended family.

During my trip to Papa's funeral, Tom would not leave me alone. He texted me made up stories that Will was sick and he was taking him to the doctor, when actually William was fine. I can't even describe what all the texts were about. They were coming in incessantly from morning until night, and I knew I had to answer them. There were times when I said, "Hey I'm hanging out with cousins and I won't be available for a little bit. If something is going on, you can handle it." He sent constant texts anyway.

I began to express annoyance to my family. "Why the fuck won't he just leave me alone?" It became a joke within the family — how many times is Tom going to text Kate? One night, we placed bets on the number of times Tom would text me over the next 24-hour period. We wrote numbers on pieces of paper and put them in a basket with names and our guesses. The next night, I counted all texts starting from the night before. There were *156 texts*. I think my uncle won. We were laughing, as a family, about this guy who was constantly texting me, not leaving me alone, even during a funeral.

It really wasn't funny though.

Talk about power, control and dominating my attention. He didn't care what I was going through, or what anyone in my family was going through. He just wanted my attention — no matter what.

And I knew I needed to give it to him. It was awful.

On the day of my grandfather's funeral, it was highly emotional. There was an open casket and everyone was bawling. We grandkids were the ones to carry the coffin from the hearse to the gravesite. We were all sobbing. I had to say very clearly to Tom before the funeral, "I am putting my phone away. I am not going to look at it for a while. You have to understand. If there is an emergency, you need to handle it."

I put my phone away. I didn't look at it.

He didn't care.

When I checked it later in the day, he had blasted my phone with nonsense. It was all a tactic to get my attention and pull it away from my family and my grandfather's funeral. I feel fortunate that I wasn't so deep into being controlled that I kept my phone out or was texting at inappropriate times to satisfy him. I drew the boundary and told him I wasn't available. He crossed it, but with my phone put away, I didn't care. That was a pattern — his attempts to control every situation whether he was directly involved or not. I didn't need Tom and he knew that. However, when I was spending time with my family, he had to continue inserting himself invasively and insensitively.

I never did tell him that he was the butt of our family joke. We all knew he was an asshole.

Chapter 20
The Predator And
The Prey

Tom had a hypnosis book on his nightstand. It's super creepy and weird when I think about it now. Although at first, I didn't see it as such. At least not in the first few months of dating.

Of all the degrees he could have earned, Tom got a master's degree in psychology. Talk about irony. But I also think he got an honorary degree in learning how to manipulate and control others. He learned how the mind works. He told me that during his education, they talked about hypnosis as a method of therapy. Maybe that was why I didn't think it was so weird that he had an interest in it. I knew people who were trained in hypnosis for therapeutic reasons. Having gone through treatment for PTSD, I now know hypnosis is often used.

We'd been dating a couple months and he asked if I wanted to try it. I never had before. I was a little interested to see if I could actually be hypnotized or not. I agreed.

I laid on his bed and closed my eyes. He grabbed the book from the nightstand drawer and read some things about getting me into a deeper place in my mind. It didn't work. I'm not sure if it was him, or if I had my guard up, or if I couldn't be hypnotized. He tried a handful of times, not in a demanding way, but rather asking me if I wanted to try it again. "There's a helium balloon and it's tied to your pointer finger and it's starting to lift up slowly," he'd say. I physically did it, kind of playing along, to placate him. Another was something about a staircase and picturing yourself walking slowly down. With each step you took you fell deeper and deeper into a sleep state. I could picture it. Even now when therapists do a similar imagery method with me, I am able to do that. But I was not hypnotized by Tom.

It was so creepy — it now makes my skin crawl. He probably did this with many different women to see who was vulnerable. To see who would go along and who would tell him to fuck off. Even though it didn't work technically with me, he was able to read my complacency to go along. I was suggestable. The fact that I would even entertain it probably gave him clues about me as a person.

It's so gross. He was studying me, as his prey.

He was the predator. And he bought bombs for the Predator while in the Air Force. It's eerie.

I should have told him he was a freak and left and never looked back — instead, fun-loving Kate said, "Oh, ok sure!" I was always up for new things. So that's what I did.

When I think about it now, it's beyond disturbing to me that he did this. And it was early in our relationship that he sought out ways to test me, to figure me out. Sometimes when I think about the fact that I went along with his nonsense, it seems like I was being brainwashed. He'd suggest things and I followed.

It's so unlike me. I'm not a follower and never have been.

Then there was this: Within the first couple times we were together, he drugged me. Literally.

On one particular night, we had some red wine. Tom fancied himself to be a connoisseur of fine wines, part of his grandiose persona. We sat outside and sipped wine, then later on went upstairs, hooked up and went to sleep. When we got up the next morning, I had to go home and get ready for work. We showered, got ready and thought we could have a quick breakfast together before he took me home. He ran to McDonald's to grab a couple breakfast sandwiches.

It was a 15-minute or so drive to my place. We got in the car after breakfast and started driving on I-395. I clearly remember looking at the road and it was starting to become wavy and fuzzy. I didn't want to tell Tom I was feeling strange. I felt a little embarrassed, thinking maybe I was hungover from the wine the night before. We got to my house. I felt all woozy. I still said nothing. I gave him a kiss goodbye and went inside.

I remember going in the house. I remember thinking there was no way I could go to work. I felt terrible and out of it. I got on my computer to email my manager and let her know I was sick. I asked her to call me if she needed anything.

That was the last thing I remembered. I was out cold. For the whole day. I'd wake up once in a while, groggy, and then I'd fall back asleep.

Finally, around 4 p.m., I started to come around. It never entered my mind that I had been drugged. I was confused. I didn't understand what happened. I thought I was really sick and hungover. I checked my email to see if my manager had responded. I read over what I wrote and thankfully it was coherent, but I gave her a completely wrong phone number.

That night, I called and told him how weird I had felt. My mind felt foggy and I asked him if I really drank that much the night before. He said, nonchalantly, "Oh well, when we were going to bed I gave you half an Ambien to help you sleep."

I didn't remember that. At all. But he made it seem like I wouldn't remember because of the wine.

When I described how the road looked to me when we were driving home and how I blacked out for the whole day he said, "Oh yeah that's definitely the Ambien. I bet it got stuck in your throat when you laid down to go to sleep and then when you stood up in the morning it went down your throat. So that's why it had an effect on you during the day."

I was like, "Oh yeah, that's probably what happened."

Slaps palm to head. I mean, really Kate?

Now I know. He gave it to me in the morning. Of course, he did. But I didn't think that was possible until I saw the real him.

He probably crushed it and put it in my McDonald's breakfast sandwich. It didn't get stuck in my throat. Something about that felt very off. Also, it wasn't like he needed to give me Ambien in order to have sex with me. We drank wine and had sex, that I remember. That right there was a sign of a straight up predator. But I didn't tell anyone about it. So there was no one else to see the red flag. Had I told people, I'm sure others would have seen it and said, "Hey, what the hell, Kate?" But I didn't tell anybody. I wanted to trust him, what he told me, and for some reason, it made sense in my head. I had wine, so I was wondering if I really did not remember what happened.

But it was gaslighting — that crazy-making, textbook behavior. He was making me question my reality of what happened. He was rewriting the script.

It remained in the back of my mind, however. I had an inkling that it didn't make a whole lot of sense. Something like that had never happened to me before. It was a moment I would remember throughout our relationship. I had a gut instinct and I completely ignored it. I went along with the story he created and sold to me.

Tom was *really* into Ambien.

In the summer of 2009, we were visiting my parents in Rockport, MA. My parents were watching the kids and Tom and I went for a hike to the granite quarry pits. The quarry pits are vast and beautiful, with natural water. We had a great time climbing around, and then went back to the house afterwards. The next morning, the top of my foot hurt. It was swollen and I showed Tom. I asked him what it could be. He suggested that maybe I had hurt it hiking, but I didn't twist it or anything.

Once home, I had some X-rays done and the military doctors kept saying they didn't see anything, it was nothing. But it continued to hurt and the swelling didn't stop. After about a month, they finally did a CAT scan. I drank a liquid that would light up areas in my foot. Lo and behold, I had several stress fractures in the tiny bones on the top of my foot. It was as if something was dropped on my foot. It definitely wasn't from hiking, which was what Tom continued saying. The doctors asked me if I dropped a can of food or something on my foot and I said no. I would have remembered doing that. I would have remembered if I did something that hurt so much to cause swelling. I had zero recollection of anything that happened to my foot, yet there were fractures.

I had to wear an orthopedic boot for six weeks and elevate my foot whenever I was sitting down. The foot healed. But I could never really shake the feeling that something was weird about the whole thing.

My theory now? He gave me Ambien and hurt my foot. Listen, everything odd that happened to me could be traced to something he did. I'd never had anything like that happen before or after. Unexplained stress fractures on my foot that I don't remember? Definitely the work of Tom Maffei.

Chapter 21
Shady Findings

Less than two weeks after the shooting, the lead detective called me and said he wanted to meet at my parents' house to talk with my dad and me. He found stuff on Tom's phone that was concerning. He didn't indicate what it was. I was definitely nervous. I never knew what to expect and could only imagine what wacko crap there could be on Tom's phone. My mind went in a million directions. But it did not go in the direction that was presented when the detective arrived.

He came in and we decided to go out on the patio and close the sliding doors. My mom was keeping William occupied in the house. The detective opened his manila folder and pulled out two printed pictures. My father and I burst into tears when we saw them. The photos were of William, at about 3 years old. One was of him on the floor, naked. His legs were bent backwards over his shoulders and his bum was in the air. The second was of him in the bathroom, with a towel draped over his shoulders — he was fully nude from the front. He looked as if he was posed. There was a strange look on his face. The detective wanted us to know they would be passing the photos on to the child pornography investigators. They would be the ones to decide if they would add child porn charges, in addition to the shooting.

Parents taking bathtub-type pictures of their kids can be normal, but you leave the genitalia out of the photo. These were weird, they were disturbing. I was worried. Ok, yeah here are these pictures, but did he do anything to William? I knew that was something I was going to have to work with William's therapist on, to find out. She had been coming in every week since the shooting.

The detective said he'd let us know the outcome of the investigation. It took a while, and I continued following up. It was frustrating. That was about my child and I wanted to know as much as possible.

I was called into the station and the detective let me know that they were not going to pursue child porn charges on Tom. The child pornography investigator thought they were, of course, borderline. Apparently, they weren't overtly-perverted enough for charges to be added.

I really wanted them to throw the book at Tom though, for him to be in even more trouble. I wanted William protected. Adding more charges onto the shooting would have buried Tom even further. But I had no control over that.

William's therapist worked with him immediately to decipher if something inappropriate had happened. William thankfully didn't give any indications that he was sexually abused by his dad, nor was he showing any signs through therapeutic play with dolls. To our relief, his therapist didn't see the markers of a child who had been violated.

I've subsequently asked him as he's gotten older, and he continues to maintain he was never inappropriately touched. He's very clear about what good touch/bad touch is. But it still hangs over me. What if he just doesn't remember? I'd put *nothing* past Tom.

Nothing surprises me anymore about Tom's behavior. It was another fixated wrinkle in the closet after being shot and almost killed. There was a possibility that Tom was sexually abusive and/or inappropriate with his own son. It was enough to alarm the police and call for an investigation. The trauma kept piling up. It was one thing after another. I couldn't stop crying when I looked at William. I was feeling so worried that something had happened to him.

Tom's a sick fuck.

Chapter 22
The Accident(s)

Part of Tom's job in the Air Force was putting contracts together for the military. Their fiscal year-end was September 30. On that entire day, the whole unit would work all the way through the stroke of midnight. They would double, triple check things, review discrepancies — it was a process the whole unit completed together. He told me about it on the days leading up to year-end and asked me to come by at some point in the evening to meet his unit. Henry was with his dad, and I agreed.

I stopped in about 7 p.m. or so and was able to meet some of the people he worked with and talked about. Tom didn't have a lot of friends, but there were a couple people he talked to regularly in his unit. One was a guy named Keith. He also made sure to introduce me to the civilian woman he said was always flirting with him. Was it an attempt to create jealousy?

Of course it was.

Those that were lower ranking or enlisted were doing a lot of the work as far as gathering the contracts and going back and forth between offices to obtain final signatures. Tom seemed to be kind of sitting back behind his desk, waiting for people to come in and he would just have to sign. He didn't seem to be part of the camaraderie of the unit, or of the work as a whole. As people would filter in and out, I met them and they were having beers. They were all friendly to me and happy to meet me.

At about 9 or 10 p.m. I knew he had to wrap things up and I decided to go back to his place. That was before I moved in and I told him I would wait up until he got home. Around 12:30 a.m., I received a call from his phone. I heard, "Kate, there's been an accident."

"Keith?" I said. The voice distinctly sounded like the guy I met earlier from Tom's unit.

He paused and said, "Oh, no. I'm calling from the side of the road. Your boyfriend's been in a motorcycle accident."

I sat up in bed. "Is he okay? Is he alive?"

"Yes," the man who sounded like Keith said. "He's alive. I went over and checked. He asked me to take his phone out and call you. But it's bad. He can't move."

Of course I started to panic. I asked for details and then I could hear sirens in the background. The guy stayed on the phone with me and then he eventually gave it over to a police officer. The officer confirmed that Tom had hit the back of a vehicle at full speed, flipped over his handlebars, over the car and landed on the ground on the Beltway.

That was it. We hung up.

I was pacing around the room. How was I going to find out which hospital? I began crying and I called my mom. "I just met this great guy, 'Mr. Fantastic,' and he was in a motorcycle accident." I didn't know if he was paralyzed, I didn't know if he was going to die and I was scared. My mom was trying to calm me. Then another call came in from the police officer who said Tom was being flown to Suburban Hospital in Bethesda, Maryland and I should meet them there.

I got dressed and jumped into my car, speeding on the Beltway. On the way, I was pulled over by a cop. I explained that my military boyfriend was in a bad accident and asked if he had heard about it. He said that he did. I told him I would slow down and he let me go.

At the hospital, I checked in at the front desk and they took me to Tom. He was on a gurney and covered in blankets. He smiled when he saw me. His arms were propped up and immobile. They did a scan before I got there. The doctor came in with the results and started listing his injuries. Both wrists were badly broken, broken fingers, he had a compound fracture near his ankle. He needed multiple surgeries and would be in the hospital for more than a week.

I blacked out.

It was a combination of the stress and I got woozy about those kinds of things. When I came to, they had placed me in a bed next to him. I said, "What good am I to you if I pass out?" We started laughing with each other. Some of the hospital staff were also taking care of me. I told Tom I wasn't going to leave him. I wanted to stay in the hospital through his surgeries. I planned to explain the situation to my boss. She had been following our whirlwind romance and was happy for me that I had found someone so great. It didn't seem like his family would be coming into town to be with him, so I wanted to be there.

Right. About his family.

Tom called his dad, who had stopped talking to him. He told him of the accident. His dad said he was stupid and shouldn't have been on the motorcycle anyway and then hung up on him. He called his mom and she was upset and crying, but she wouldn't travel out of New Jersey to see her son who was in a motorcycle accident and could have died.

He had no one.

I called Henry's dad and told him what happened and asked if Henry could stay with him for the week because I wanted to be at the hospital, and he agreed. I had all my bases covered. I stayed with him for four or five days while he was going in and out of surgeries and recoveries.

During that time a lot of weirdness happened.

As he was coming out of one of the surgeries, the nurse pulled me aside and asked me if Tom had herpes. I was like, "What? No, not to my knowledge." She said, "Well, there's a big sore on his penis." I went and looked and there was a round wound on it. I didn't say anything as he was coming out of surgery. I waited till later. I didn't even say herpes. I asked if he saw what was on him.

Tom looked and he said, "Oh yeah, I remember when I hit the car, my junk smashed into the front of the bike. It was like a jolt and then I hit." He was saying that whatever was on his penis had to do with the accident. That was hard to believe, but at the time I accepted it was a wound from the accident.

He was a mess. His leg and both his arms were in traction. He was on a lot of morphine. He had all kinds of compression stuff for blood clots. The goal was to get him up and walking daily, to promote circulation. A few days after the accident, the nurse came in and got him up and he was able to limp enough to navigate the hallway with a bit with help. I offered to help him. When he got up, the nurse didn't tie the back of his gown. I was focused on supporting his arm and propping him up and I didn't notice it either.

All of the sudden, he looked at me with this face of hatred and said, "You're trying to embarrass me."

"What are you talking about?" I asked.

"You did this on purpose so people could see my naked ass," he retorted.

I didn't realize his ass was exposed. I quickly went around and tied the gown.

Then he escalated, "You can just get the fuck out of here. You tried to embarrass me. Just go fucking home, I don't even want to see you."

The nurse was standing right there. I looked at her. She looked at me and my face became red and my eyes teared up.

"No, I didn't," I said. "I didn't do anything. I didn't even know it was open."

"Just fucking go," he muttered.

I'd never seen him like that before. I was flustered and rattled and hurt.

I grabbed my stuff and went downstairs. I sat on the bench and cried. I called Natasha and told her what happened. I had to tell someone. I don't remember what she said, but I know I decided to go back up to his room and see if I could smooth things over.

It was the one and only time he didn't act as if nothing happened. Maybe he saw the look on my face. He knew he had to pull the mask back on and reel me in again. He blamed it on the morphine. He was in pain and was not himself. But I did see in that moment exactly who he was. That was the same face I saw many times later when his behavior escalated. The same face I saw at the shooting. He was showing me his inner psychopath. He used the accident, the pain and the medicine as an excuse. There was always an excuse.

Immediately, I forgave him. Of course that made sense. He wasn't himself, he was in a serious accident and I understood that.

The following day, he said, "Kate, you're a good girl. I knew you were a keeper the minute that you dropped everything to be by my side. You could have abandoned me. You could have not cared about what happened. But you're a good person, you're a good girl. There's something for you in the closet back at my house. Go home, go into the little cubbies in my closet, the ones where my socks are, and you'll find a little box."

I knew. He must have already bought a ring. Maybe he was planning to ask me in Mexico? We had been talking about getting engaged since we planned our trip, and we started talking about marriage quickly. The accident was on October 1 and we knew we wouldn't be able to go to Mexico later in October as we originally planned. Those plans would be pushed to December.

It's hard to explain how I felt driving to pick up my own engagement ring.

I can't say I was giddy. I wasn't giddy. I wasn't nervous either. I did think it was a little odd, that he already had the ring, that we hadn't gone to pick one out together. How long had he had it sitting in his closet? We'd only been together three months. But I did as told, found the box, and hopped back in my car.

When I got back to his room, he told me to give him the box. "Close your eyes," he said. "Now open them." He had the nurse open the box because he couldn't use his broken wrists. "Will you marry me?"

I yelled, "Yes!" and put the ring on my finger, just staring at it. The nurse was hugging us both and clapping and brought other nurses in and made a big deal. They thought it was so romantic, this military guy who was hurt and me who stuck by his side. It was a romantic story and people ate it up.

Including me.

I called to tell my parents. They were shocked. But as my parents did, they rolled with me. They could hear how happy I was and they hadn't even met him yet. I was ecstatic. I had the nurse take a bunch of pictures.

I was going to marry Tom Maffei.

Chapter 23
Anti-Social Behavior

A year to a year and one-half into our relationship, when we lived in Fort Belvoir, the incessant texting began while my parents were visiting. We didn't see each other regularly since they had moved to Florida, so when they came to our house, they would stay a few days to a week. We would talk, tell funny stories, share a bottle of wine and catch up on life.

Tom was not down with that.

He would take care of all the cooking. Actually, he always took care of the cooking. I wasn't allowed to cook. The kitchen was his. We would sit down and have dinner together. He would stay in the living room afterwards for a short amount of time, but not engaging at all. He'd be browsing Amazon or surfing the web on his phone. He kept to himself. Then he would complain about his back hurting and go upstairs. Every time.

I would tell him I would be up later, that I was going to stay downstairs with my parents. But once he was upstairs, he would begin texting me. Bugging me. "When are you coming up? It's getting late." I never went up until I was ready. I didn't comply. Sometimes he tried to be funny, just trying to get a response. Other times he would tell me about something he was watching on TV. It was to draw my attention away from my parents and back onto him.

Another time my parents were at our house in Fort Belvoir. We had been getting a meal delivery of fresh foods to prepare and I really wanted to cook for my parents. I told him to let me do it and he didn't like that. Tom threw a fit, like a toddler having a tantrum. A baby, not getting his needs met. He stormed out the back door as I was standing in the kitchen talking to my mom and making the meal. It was awkward — we just looked at each other. But I kept moving forward. I finished the meal and served everyone. He was texting me during dinner. He said, "I can see you. I'm just out back. I'm watching you. You don't even care that I left. Yeah, go ahead and enjoy that meal."

After dinner, he came back into the house and said hi to everyone and acted as if nothing had happened. I was expected to sweep it under the rug, without making anyone uncomfortable.

I was constantly tiptoeing around like that, walking on eggshells. I just wanted peace. I wanted calm. Responding to his texts was a way to achieve that. If I didn't, I knew it would create a mess. It was stressful, sitting there with my parents, wanting to give them attention, knowing I had to have my phone with me to answer the texts he was sending me from upstairs. My parents were watching me. I knew it was rude. I hated it.

When we moved to Florida, we would visit my parents at their house. If he didn't cause a scene, he would be off, not interacting with the family. Even when my brother and his family were there, Tom would be in another room, by himself, texting me. By the time we moved to Florida, I stopped caring. I stopped caring that he didn't interact with my family. I was hanging out with my family and I was fine. I'm sure that was why he felt threatened by my family. I didn't care what he thought. I left him alone and did my own thing. I knew he didn't like that, but I didn't care anymore.

My parents really did try with him. They are very warm and welcoming. They wanted to accept Tom into our family. They gave him lots of chances and they were always supportive.

That's who they are. They are happy when their kids are loved, safe, supported and happy themselves. They spent a lot of time with Henry and Will, and loved being grandparents to them. They wanted goodness for me, Henry and Will.

Before the shooting, my dad expressed concerns to me about Tom's pain pill usage. He brought up the fact that Tom would go upstairs and text me. And the fact that he created drama at family gatherings. He thought some of his behaviors were very strange.

Did they know Tom very well? Not really. Tom didn't offer much. He was closed off, by design. No one — knew him well. He didn't say much about himself or his life or childhood, other than minor anecdotes about his father being pretty tough, especially with his brothers. He hit them. He said his father was a pilot in the military and then flew for American Airlines. He said that he cheated on his mom. That his mom was sweet but passive.

He never said anything about his dad being abusive towards his mom. But I'd put money down on that.

As a result of everything that happened, my father said we only saw the tip of the iceberg with Tom. We didn't really know who he was and all that he was doing. He was shady.

My mom was a momma bear. Once Tom screwed with us, she was done with him. That was before the shooting. She tolerated the time I went back with him. She loved me and the kids and would never turn her back on us. She was probably afraid to turn her back because she didn't know what Tom would do.

It was a pattern, closing himself off to others, including my parents. He didn't go out of his way to know them or spend time with people I cared about. It was a red flag.

Chapter 24
Military Mistakes

Colonel Travis Adams had no idea his soldier had moved away from Virginia and down to Florida. He really had no idea. He thought Tom was stuck doing physical therapy because of his back and still hooked on pain pills. Tom never went to work and his commander never checked on him. That wouldn't fly in any other place of employment, not that I know of. Tom literally left Virginia. He wasn't going to Andrews Air Force Base. He wasn't going into work. Adams never held him accountable.

I knew Tom was lying to his commander and the military. But I couldn't stop Tom from doing any of his nefarious shit.

The day after I got a restraining order against Tom for spousal abuse, I emailed his commander. I scanned the PDF that Tom created — the fake orders to move our belongings from Virginia to Florida. I scanned the restraining order, too, and emailed the papers to Colonel Adams. I told him, so he would know that Thomas had not been in Virginia for three months, that he'd been in Florida with me, with his family. "The military moved all of our stuff, here's the document that was used," I wrote. "I also need to report him for spousal abuse and here's the restraining order."

Oh how naive I was. I thought the military was honorable. Tom did illegal things — I thought he would be held accountable. People in the military can get court martialed for infidelity. What about spousal abuse?

Adams' response was vanilla.

And then I realized that he knew he couldn't say much because his head could roll for not knowing where his soldier was. He set up a call with me within an hour of receiving my email.

He was gruff. He turned the blame to me. "Why didn't you report this sooner?" I told him Tom did what Tom wanted to do. That was his idea. He did it. Tom told me nothing would happen to him, that the military would never know. I said my account of abuse was warranted and a civilian judge granted a temporary restraining order. He then told me that Thomas was on the road, headed back to Virginia. At that point, I knew that Adams had contacted Tom.

He was still in active duty. He was AWOL. On top of everything else.

My good friend Monique, who lived next door to us at Fort Belvoir, knew the ins and outs of the military very well. She knew who to point me to in order to go above the command. She found contact information for the Office of Special Investigation (OSI), the military's version of the FBI. She was very helpful to me — I'd never have known who to go to in the military without her. I made contact with OSI and gave them the same materials as I gave the commander. I was assigned an investigator. They had investigators come to my house and they seized our computer he used to make the fraudulent document. It was a full-fledged investigation, not only on the fraud but also on spousal abuse.

During that time, the military tacked on another restraining order, along with the civilian one. They held Tom at Bolling Air Force Base, and he had someone he had to check in with twice a day. The commander let me know the details, as did OSI. I felt somewhat better because he was contained by the military. He was a gigantic bully and thought he was above the law in every way, but he wasn't going to fuck around with the military.

He was moved out from under Adams and was assigned to a different commander, Mel Robbins. She then became my liaison. My guess is they were trying to protect Adams and remove him from the Tom Maffei situation. Wouldn't want him to get in trouble, now would we?

The scariest part was the military actually *lost* Tom.

More than once.

I got a call from his commander that morning and she told me that Tom didn't check in and he wasn't answering his phone. "We don't know where he is. For your safety, you, your son and your parents should go to a hotel. We don't know where he is, we don't know if he's still in the area or if he's back in Florida, but you need to take steps to protect yourselves." We went into hiding in a hotel in Coral Springs, Florida for two days. I was still working at the time. With every step, I had to let my manager know what was happening. I was working out of the hotel room. We were terrified, looking over our shoulders and I *still* had to work.

This is why women get fired during abusive relationships. This is why women lose their livelihood over men behaving badly.

For almost 48 hours, the military couldn't find him. Then later on day two I received a call from his commander that he was found. Their story was that he checked into Walter Reed for a "psych issue." The doctor forgot to either put down his information or forgot to contact his command. I really didn't believe the excuses they gave. Yeah, fucking right. A guy goes AWOL and is in the confines of a military hospital and you didn't know about it? They lost him and didn't take responsibility for it.

That was the first time they lost him. The second time was shorter, but we were still alerted and we went to a hotel again. He hadn't checked in one morning and he made an excuse as to why. Once they found him, we left the hotel and it was like, "Ok, oops, no biggie, just go live your lives again."

The handling of his case was horrendous. It left a bad taste in my mouth about the military. Since then, I haven't celebrated any military holidays. Some will find this offensive or blasphemous but — after what they put me through, and how they covered for their guy? Nope.

So the investigation started in January. A couple of months later in March, I received a call from the lead investigator at OSI. The investigation was complete. They found him guilty of fraud and spousal abuse. They told me they were recommending court martial and turning the case over to his command, who would be making the decision on what to do.

"What do you mean it goes to his command?" I said. "Um, they'd found him GUILTY!"

"Yes, that's the protocol in the military. The command decides what to do with him," the investigator said.

They did a full-blown investigation, found him guilty and were recommending to the command that he be court martialed. But that would not guarantee that a court martial would happen? "What do you mean?" I pushed. "It's up to the command," he responded.

I held onto faith that they would do the right thing. After all, the military is full of honorable people, right? There are rules, strict consequences. This guy had defrauded the government!

Then I received a call from Mel Robbins. She was very short and curt. She informed me that they decided not to court martial Tom, that they would be handling it "administratively", and that they planned to retire him immediately.

It took my breath away.

I said, "M'am, the military has to hold him accountable. You need to keep us safe, he's dangerous. If you just retire him, he's going to come back down here and I don't know what he's going to do."

She didn't give a shit. She kept repeating that they were handling it administratively. She added that they didn't want him to lose his pension for serving for 25 years. Apparently, that took precedence over being fraudulent and dangerous.

They retired him to get their bad soldier out of their hair.

"If he comes after us, you will have blood on your hands," I said.

By the way, those commanders can kiss my ass. They should be fired from whatever high profile position they have. Oh, and I emailed them his mug shot and media articles from the shooting, and "thanked" them for keeping us safe from their soldier.

Of course they didn't respond. Complicit cowards.

Chapter 25
"Crazy Wife" Deflect

Within two and one-half years of our relationship, the abuse escalated from power, control, and emotional abuse to physical threats. I had convinced Tom a year earlier that I could be active on Facebook and only have male contacts that were family members. I stuck to it. But I could see posts from other people I was acquainted with. In the beginning of the New Year 2011, I was on Facebook and I saw a funny comment on a post from a guy I went to high school with. Tom and Henry were playing video games and when I walked into the room I was laughing. Tom asked what I was laughing about and I told him something I read on Facebook.

He replied, "Oh it's probably from a guy." And I could tell it was going to escalate from there. He said it in front of Henry, too. I asked if we could just not argue about that because I had to get up early to take Henry to the airport. But he said, "Forget it, I'm leaving."

He stormed out of the house, and immediately began blowing up my phone with texts and emails. He texted later that he was at a strip club and there were so many hot women around him. I was so exhausted from his behavior, I really didn't even care. I *wanted* him to find someone else to be with and I didn't give a shit about it. He sent me a picture of a sign outside a strip club, saying he was so drunk. He didn't stop, for hours. At 2 a.m., he texted that he was coming home. I told him not to. I said, "If you're that drunk, then I don't want you in this house."

Of course, he didn't listen to me.

I was in our bedroom and I heard him come through the interior garage door. I got up and walked out of the room and he stormed past me, into the bedroom and shut the door. I was standing near the door and I heard a "click click" — the indistinguishable sound of the chambering of a gun.

"Oh fuck, he's going to shoot me," I panicked. "I have to get outside so if he does, someone will hear it and help me." I turned around and ran through the house, ran out the front door, and called 911. I'd just finished giving my address and telling the operator that my husband and I had had a fight and I thought he had a gun, when I looked to the side of me and noticed the garage door had opened. Tom walked out holding 2-year-old William, still in his sleep sack. He proceeded to get into the car and put William on his lap. Not in a car seat, not restrained, but on his lap.

I had a moment of "WHAT DO I DO?" Henry was in the house sleeping, but Tom was about to leave with Will. Instinctively I jumped into the car. I was still on the phone with 911. I was screaming that he had a gun, he was taking my baby. Tom grabbed my phone, ended the call, and threw it on the car floor. He peeled out of the driveway and sped up the street. At the end of the block he stopped the car and raised his fist. He said, "GET OUT OF THE FUCKING CAR OR I'M GOING TO PUNCH YOU IN YOUR FUCKING FACE!!" and moved his fist towards me to let me know he was serious. Shocked and knowing he meant it, I jumped out of the car and slammed the door.

He went tearing around the corner and back up the street. As I stood on the corner, I saw the tail lights as he put the car in reverse, apparently having decided to come back after me. I jumped into some nearby bushes, shaken to my core — I lost complete control of my bladder. He couldn't see me and so he turned the corner on to the next street. I immediately started running down the street screaming, "He's got my baby, somebody please help me!" I knocked on doors and went up to houses that looked like there were lights on but no one answered my cries.

I knew I had called 911 and I hoped the police had arrived at my house. I decided to go back — in addition to everything else, Henry was still there sleeping.

I ran up the street towards the house. I had urine all down the front of me, I was crying hysterically and traumatized. And there was Tom, standing in the driveway with his stupid military coins, buddying up to the cops and handing them out. The units in the military create their own set of coins. They trade unit coins among each other and they are collectibles. Tom had a ton and used them to impress others.

Tom got to the house before the police. He put William back into the crib and I couldn't prove anything that went down. He also managed to grab a handful of coins to give the police. I could tell by the way they were looking at me that they thought I was the problem. I knew exactly what Tom was doing and they completely fell for it.

One officer asked me to go inside. He had me call my parents. I screamed into the phone, "COME GET US!" when my mom answered. I can only imagine her terror.

That officer also told me that he'd seen enough "domestics" to know that if Tom didn't hit me that time, he would next time. He advised me to get a restraining order at the courthouse the next day. The police also told me that I had to leave the house with the children, because Tom had nowhere else to go. So they made me wake up Henry and get Will back out of his crib and go to my parents' house. My parents came to pick me up and they were horrified upon learning of the events.

The police! Why would they make the mother and children leave the home? Make him leave! He had money! He had plenty of it! He could go to a hotel! Maybe they thought we were safer with my parents? Who knows. I didn't sleep at all. We basically got to my parents and an hour later I had to leave to put Henry on a plane. I don't know how I did it. I was shaking, my stomach was bottoming out, and I was in shock. I was cold with chills all over my body.

My dad went with me to the airport. It was always hard to put Henry on a plane. He was little. It was horrendous. No mother should ever have to do that. I was trying to stay calm. Somehow, I did it. I got him on the plane. I'd been through the biggest trauma at that point in my entire life, and add to it putting my young child on a plane.

Afterwards, my dad and I went directly to the courthouse and applied for a restraining order. I was still shaking and in shock.

Chapter 26
Temporary
Restraining Order

The dark paneled hallway was long with benches on both sides of it. There were plenty of times when a woman seeking a restraining order at Broward County Courthouse had to wait on the bench across from her abuser. Not exactly a safe setup. That significant detail was never considered.

The morning after Tom drove off with our son and threatened to punch me in the face, I put Henry on an airplane to go back to his dad. Then my father and I went to that old-school government building in an attempt to keep Tom away from us. The people behind the glass who handed me the paperwork to file for a restraining order looked at me with zero emotion. It was as robotic as going to the Department of Motor Vehicles.

I was still traumatized, shaking from head to toe, cold, and struggled to breathe. I didn't even know exactly what to say or do. They buzzed me through a locked door, into a dim room, to a cubby with a chair to provide some privacy. The carpet was old and gross, the high ceilings had water stains. There was a woman there to hand my paperwork to once it was complete. She was not an advocate though. There was no assistance provided to help fill out the forms or to walk me through the many pages. I couldn't think straight. I didn't know if I was answering the questions correctly. It was a confusing and intimidating process. I'm sure that is why so many women are denied a restraining order because it's overwhelming and difficult to understand. They don't know what to write or to check off this box or that one.

Still, I filled it out. I'm a writer, so I included many details. I was clear about the gun, and that I heard the round of bullets forced into the chamber. I said Tom tried to steal our son and he threatened to punch me in my face. I handed the papers to the clerk and she informed me the judge would review all the restraining orders from the day and have a decision by 4 pm. It was early in the morning when I filed my report. I'd have to wait all day long to find out if it was approved or denied.

My dad and I drove back to Parkland. I was in a fog of shock and disbelief from the trauma, anxiety and uncertainty I was experiencing.

My dad took me back later that afternoon to a waiting area in the domestic violence division. Other women were sitting there as well. A couple of them had kids who were fussing. Each time the clerk came into the room with paperwork in her hands, my anticipation rose to hear my name. Finally it was my turn. The restraining order was granted. She explained that I was to keep one packet with the temporary restraining order on me at all times, so I could show it in case he violated it. I was instructed to give the other packet to the Parkland Broward County Sheriff's Office. They would then serve the order to Tom.

My dad and I went straight to Parkland BSO where I met with a deputy and gave him the packet. He asked me if Tom had weapons and I told them he had many. He asked me what kinds. I informed him of the two big shotguns, several handguns, and some air rifles. I told him where the safes were. He told us that under Florida law, they could seize all the weapons in the house once Tom was served.

He explained that they would get in touch with me that evening, when they would be attempting to serve him. We got the call at about 7 p.m. They instructed us to come back to the station since they were about to serve him. We followed the police cars into the neighborhood, and parked nearby where we could see the house. I was bawling my eyes out. I couldn't believe that was happening.

Actually, it happened quickly. All of a sudden, we saw Tom's BMW as he turned the corner and then he sped off because cop cars were in our driveway. He knew why they were there — why else would he take off? Other officers barricaded him at the end of the street, with their lights on and they served him there. I was so scared about all of it. It was truly terrifying. I never thought that would be my life in my mid-30s. I'd never had to deal with any criminal-type stuff with police and courts. It was gut wrenching.

It felt like I was being ripped apart.

After they served him, they were able to go into the house. They confirmed they removed the weapons I described.

But in the next sentence, they told me he could go out and buy another gun tomorrow. Legally, there was nothing stopping him from buying another weapon.

My blood went cold. What the fuck???

I did the things I was advised to do. I left. I got a restraining order to protect myself and my child. But Tom could go and get *another* gun if he wanted to? What about common sense gun laws? There's one right there. Abusers escalate the most when the woman leaves and the man is served a restraining order. Yet, men can still have access to guns? It's senseless. And it is deadly.

Chapter 27
Stalking And
Harassing

During the eight months of the temporary restraining order — that was never made permanent by our Family Court judge — Tom continued to walk the line of harassing and stalking me. Unfortunately, I was never able to prove anything, with one exception. After January, when he drove off with Will and threatened to punch me, I was traumatized and didn't feel safe living in our home together. I chose to go to my parents' house. We had this brand new beautiful home sitting empty because he was AWOL and went back to Virginia, and I felt William and I were safer with my parents. After several months, my divorce attorney urged me to move back into the marital home. He had his eyes set on me getting the home. Since Tom was back in Virginia, under lock and key with the military, it should have been fine.

I talked with my parents and we decided that would be the plan. After coordinating with the Parkland police, they flagged my home in their system because of the domestic violence history. I felt safe knowing people were watching out for me and were prepared to respond. We installed an alarm system in the home. I wore the panic fob button on me at all times. Literally. The only exception was when I was in the shower and even then it was within reach. If I pressed it, it would go directly to the Parkland BSO and the deputies would respond. I took the necessary steps.

At one point, after the military retired Tom and I didn't know where he was, he broke into the marital home.

My dad had gone into the house to get something for me when I was at work. He called the police immediately, took pictures, texted them to me, then called me. The interior garage door had been hacked. There were chop marks on the door. The frame was off the hinges. We couldn't figure out how Tom did that. I had changed the locks. There were no signs of a breaking and entering. Then we noticed my garage door had been tampered with. The connection to the automatic door was dangling down. It must have occurred when he left the home months prior to his return to Virginia. I never parked in the garage so I didn't notice it. I always kept the interior door locked. So he was basically able to manually lift the garage door because of the broken electrical connection.

At that point he got through the interior door by hacking and chopping at it. There was nothing taken from the house. There was nothing out of place. He wanted me to know he could still get to me.

That was the message.

I reminded the police that I had a restraining order and he couldn't be near me, even at the house. It literally said he couldn't be within 500 feet of the home, with the address listed.

They said we were both on the deed and it was technically still his house too. And technically I wasn't home at the time, allowing him the right to go into his own home. They were not going to arrest him. "But what if I *was* home?" I asked. "Well that would be a different story," they said, "but you're weren't home. It's his home too and there's nothing we can do."

He got away with it.

For a brief time after that, running with fear from the marital home and not feeling safe, I moved into a two-bedroom apartment in a gated community, across the canal from my parents' house. I could see their house from my balcony.

I lived there maybe two months.

On one particular day, I was working from home and had to run an errand. I came back to the apartment and went in. Will was still at preschool. I walked up the stairs and I sensed that something was off. It was that feeling you get when your Spidey senses start tingling.

I went into my bedroom and found the screen was off and resting against the sliding glass door. The door was ajar. It was one of those moments when I asked myself whether I had left it that way or not. I considered that I'd left the door open perhaps, but definitely hadn't taken the screen off. As I surveyed the house, however, nothing seemed to be missing or out of place.

Then I went into William's room.

I could see a large, faint image on the wall. As I stepped closer, I realized it was an oversized sketch of a penis. It was drawn with a black light marker, so in the sunlight, only an outline was visible. It spanned the length of William's bed and underneath the penis it said, "HOLLA!"

My stomach dropped. I knew it was him.

I called the police in Coral Springs. Three of them came, and dusted for fingerprints. They got a partial fingerprint on the sliding glass door. They took pictures of the phallic symbol on the wall. (*It was disturbing that he drew it on our son's wall!*) Clearly by using black light ink, he was hoping I would go in there at night and the penis would glow on the wall. Combined with "HOLLA," it was again, another disturbing message meant for me.

Needless to say, the fingerprints came back inconclusive. The Coral Springs Police Department had also interviewed some of my neighbors and one reported seeing a black MDX, which was what he was driving at the time, in the driveway in front of my apartment. They described him but could not identify him in a picture. It wasn't enough to stick.

They couldn't prove it was him. Again, nothing happened. I had a restraining order and he was violating it, but I couldn't prove it.

I contacted the leasing office and told them my home was broken into and that I was out of there. I moved out immediately and went back to stay with my parents.

Tom was relentless. He created a fake Facebook profile, with the name Brett Evens. It was a photo of a handsome looking guy. He friend requested me. It pricked my suspicions right away because his ex-wife's last name was Evans. As soon as I saw Evens, I knew it was Tom. I knew. He was trying to contact me.

I made a plan to catch him.

I contacted my friend Jen, a private investigator whom I've known most of my life. I asked if she thought she could get him. She was on it. She created a fake Facebook profile of her own. She included a picture of a young, attractive woman, and she friend requested some of the same people from Brett Evens' page. She lured him into chatting with her. Both fake profiles were chatting on Messenger, but Tom didn't know he was actually messaging Jen. She flirted with him, and the dumbass actually gave her his email address. They began emailing back and forth and she asked for pictures of him. He sent her photos of himself in uniform, bragging about being in the military and telling her he has a crazy stalker ex-wife, which was why he was hiding behind a fake profile.

We gathered all of it as evidence.

I called the police again. They said the judges are hit and miss as far as actually doing something about the restraining order violations. Sometimes they enforce them, sometimes they don't (WHAT THE

FUCK?!?! DO YOUR JOBS!), but they agreed to file a full report to submit as a restraining order violation.

The violation was processed. The judge turned it down.

He said there was not enough evidence. We were able to prove that Brett Evens was really Tom Maffei and Tom Maffei had directly contacted me.

THAT is how people get away with cyber stalking. The judge didn't care that Tom did it. He thought it was stupid and petty. *He blew it off.*

Then, through both of our lawyers, Tom let them know he was sending me a child support payment through the mail, so I could expect it. A couple days later, I received a package. It was in Tom's handwriting and it was addressed to Tom, not to me. I was wondering why he sent it to himself but I was told to expect a child support payment, so I opened it. The package was packed with Valentine's Day cards with handwritten messages from Tom to me. And from me to Tom — he bought cards that he said he wished had been from me to him, and wrote notes to himself in them, as if it was me. They were devoid of emotion and they were manipulative.

"You are my partner, my love, and my very best friend — my one and only Valentine. Happy Valentine's Day." Then he hand wrote, "I will always protect you. Never lay a finger on you."

Also, no check.

I called the police *again*. When they saw the cards, they were in disbelief at Tom's infinite attempts to contact me. They did a report and again, the judge blew it off, saying it was addressed to Tom, not to me, and I shouldn't have opened the envelope. Right. I was only made aware though our attorneys that I could expect a child support payment, but I shouldn't have opened the envelope from Tom.

It was in the restraining order — he wasn't supposed to contact me in any way. Yet, the judge said it wasn't a direct threat. Tom knew just how to harass me in a way to get to me without getting the books thrown at him

Finally, *finally*, he wound up crossing a line as far as the judge was concerned, and he was arrested.

He emailed the CEO and several VPs of the national healthcare company I was working for at the time. The subject line read: Rogue Employee. He went on to give them my name, telling them they had a rogue employee on their hands. He claimed that I was drinking and sleeping during the work day, and they would want to investigate me. The email went to Human Resources and HR sent it to my manager, who immediately assured them she was in touch with me all day long, every work day. She gave them my stellar performance records. She told them I was having difficulties with my ex-husband, as I had been filling her in all along. I could have easily been fired five times over with the incessant drama of my dissolving marriage. I was fortunate to have had a manager who was supportive.

We provided the judge with the email at the next temporary restraining order hearing. Tom was arrested in the courtroom for violating it.

Yeah, big deal. He bailed out the next morning at 4 a.m. and went along his merry way. It didn't seem to phase him.

He was held accountable once but it was barely a slap on the wrist. The system failed me. They didn't take his behavior seriously. They thought I was being dramatic.

No, Tom didn't come right out and say, "I'm going to fucking kill you." But his behaviors proved he was going to extremes to continuously harass me. It was a pattern. He walked the line enough to instill fear in me and without getting caught. He blurred the lines. He knew exactly what he was doing.

Abusive men need to be held accountable and it's not happening enough. We have to begin by exposing Family Courts and judges for the inhumane way they treat women and families.

Chapter 28
Divorce Attempt #1

After I received the temporary restraining order, I was told that we would have a hearing scheduled two to three weeks later. We could request to make it permanent. I let my lawyer know from the start I wanted it permanent. I didn't trust Tom and I feared him. I felt his behavior had been escalating and that would not be a one-time offense.

When we went to the hearing a couple weeks later, we were assigned to Judge Karl Roberto in the Family Court Division. Criminal court kicked our restraining order hearing to Family Court because we had initiated divorce. The judge heard from each of us. It was a nerve-wracking and traumatizing experience. I had faith in my first attorney. He came recommended by someone I knew and he seemed to genuinely care.

Tom had hired a slimy, sleazebag attorney. He was repugnant. Lester Daniel. He blamed me in every possible way. He said I was a bad mother, claimed I drank too much, said I didn't make enough income, accused me of talking to guys on Facebook and being unfaithful. He glared at me. It was infuriating to sit there and listen to that. They were lying their asses off and making false accusations!

Tom had his smug demeanor on full display and I couldn't say anything.

The court hearing went quickly. My lawyer did a decent job of recounting the incident in the car with William, explaining that I feared for my life and we were seeking a permanent restraining order. The judge decided he was going to extend the temporary for another three months.

This would continue for the entire eight to nine-month period I was separated from Tom. We'd go in front of the judge when the temp was expiring, ask for a permanent, and he'd extend the temp. Frustrated, I asked my attorney why the judge just wouldn't make it permanent. He said he believed the problem was that Tom and I would have to co-parent eventually. So the judge was hoping the two of us could be civil and communicate for the sake of our child.

It was my first experience with someone I thought could help, but failed at identifying manipulative, abusive behavior. When women and children are in danger and getting away from an abuser, *co-parenting is not possible*. You cannot co-parent with an abuser. The court system needs to be educated to handle co-parenting in an abusive relationship.

In each hearing, my lawyer tried to explain my position, but the judge continued saying his hope was that we would be civil and work it out. That's not how it works with abusers. Their desire for power and control over their victims makes it absolutely impossible to successfully "work it out." Judges need to know this and understand that the safety of women and children supersedes an abuser's biological link to his children.

Then there was the final hearing.

So remember the part where the judge had Tom arrested at one of the hearings for having contacted my employer to get me fired? I recall that as the handcuffs were being put on him, the judge caught my eye. He nodded at me. It was very subtle, but he did.

About a week after that court hearing, I received word from my attorney that the judge recused himself from the case. He stepped down and passed it on to a different judge.

At the time, I wasn't given a reason why, nor was he required to give one. Later Tom told me that he and his attorney noticed that the judge nodded at me. I have a feeling that his attorney made threats to the judge that he showed bias and the judge recused himself.

That took place just before I decided to take Tom back.

Yes, I made one last attempt in the marriage with Tom again.

Imagine everything I was going through. Going back and forth to court several times to make the restraining order permanent, and none of it worked. By that time my parents had put in $20-25k in legal fees just fighting for the restraining order, never mind the divorce — and we barely had gotten that going yet. We ran out of money. My first lawyer dropped me. As soon as I asked to do monthly payments he dropped my case, without warning. He told me he could no longer represent me.

I was out of money, my parents could no longer help with legal fees, and the judge stepped down. I was ripe for manipulation, to get reeled back into a relationship with him. I felt completely hopeless. I felt I lost trying to make it on my own. It was proven to me very early that the system did not support or protect victims. Things didn't play out the way I expected them to. I was naive. I thought I was doing what I needed to do. Only now do I know better.

There needs to be continuing education in the Family Court system, particularly judges, with regards to how they handle domestic violence situations. Too often, abusers skate by and continue to manipulate women through the system. The judges show bias to men and it's detrimental to the children. If a man shows violence towards the mother of his children, he sure as hell is showing he can be violent to his kids and society at large. We need more harsh consequences when women come forward to judges and beg for restraining orders. Let's make the men prove that they are no longer violent. They should have to prove it. The responsibility should not be on the women to prove the man is continuing to be a threat, that is backwards and fucked up.

Chapter 29
The Reconciliation

In the summer of 2011, after nine months of going back and forth to court over a restraining order that had not been made permanent, my very expensive car was repossessed. We hadn't made a mortgage payment since January, on our new house in Parkland. That was when the shit hit the fan and Tom stopped paying his portion on our house. I couldn't afford the $2500 a month mortgage, along with Will's preschool, all the other bills, and the credit card debt. You know, the credit cards that I took out in my name to furnish the house to feel I was making a contribution to our family.

I felt vulnerable. I felt alone. My parents who always spend their summers in Massachusetts, were away. I was still working at the large healthcare company, from home. I was isolated without coworkers and without being established in Parkland long enough to make friends there. It was Will and me alone, a lot. I felt incredibly depressed.

I wish I could remember exactly how Tom and I started talking again. But I don't. Some details you choose to forget. Knowing our patterns, it began again over text or email. He was nervous to talk to me because we still had the temporary restraining order in place.

One night he said, "It was a big misunderstanding." He downplayed the physical altercation scene and told me I misinterpreted his actions — getting in the car with William, threatening to punch me. He claimed he had a momentary lapse in judgment. There was absolute refusal that he chambered the gun when locking me out of the master bedroom. He denied having a gun in the car when he took William. I was the one who didn't hear it right. It wasn't as big of a deal as I had made it out to be.

I second-guessed myself. I second-guessed my own memories of the events.

It was gaslighting. It was textbook gaslighting that only now I can recognize. The abusive partner convinces the other that it was all in her head. Tom made me think I was wrong. His chosen method of delivery wasn't in an accusatory, wagging his finger kind of way. He was humble. He pointed out how I reported him to the military, how he almost lost his career. How I had played a part in that too. I took it way too far, I overreacted, and he told me. Even when he was AWOL, he didn't come after me, surely he wasn't a threat to me. He missed Will. He wanted to be a family again.

He let me in on the government contract job he went to work for in Seattle after he retired. He had been living in a cottage off a main house there. It was overlooking the water and he said it was beautiful. He wanted Will and me to come and stay with him. He said he was clean, he was no longer taking pills. He kicked the habit and even offered to take a urine test in front of me. He sent pictures of the place. He talked about the woman who lived in the main house, how she gave him jars of homemade jellies. He painted the image of the perfect life. I wouldn't have to work, I could stay home and raise William. It would be peaceful and we could begin a beautiful new chapter in Seattle. I began having fantasies of starting our life over again. Maybe we could do a trial run in Florida? If it went well, we could make plans to relocate to Seattle.

We talked more and more. Eventually, I agreed to get back together with him. He planned to take a leave of absence from his job in Seattle and come back to Florida to reconcile. He drove and showed up five days later. I remember him pulling up in the driveway. He was even more suntanned than usual and he had dyed the top of his hair a strawberry blonde, while the rest of it remained his natural dirty-blonde. I thought he looked odd, but nevertheless I burst into tears and hugged him. He put on a smile — but he felt as cold as a glass of ice.

Telling my friends and family that I had reconciled with Tom was difficult. My parents were not happy and they let me know it. They were on the receiving end of the phone call in January that they needed to come and get us because of what Tom had done. Followed by the subsequent months of stalking and harassing. Then I was telling them that I was reconciling and getting back with him. I kept repeating to everyone that I just wanted my family back together. Tom promised that he would not take drugs anymore and he wasn't abusive — it was only that one incident. I was parroting what Tom said to me.

My people were livid. My friends were vocal about feeling worried for my safety. They didn't trust him. I was fortunate that no one turned their back on me, however. There was no shaming.

My friends and family knew that I was headstrong, that I did what I wanted. When I made a decision that was what I was going to follow through with.

We were back together for about three or four weeks and I was telling my parents, who were still in Massachusetts, about the Seattle vision. They swayed me from moving. I said, "Well, we'll see how it goes." The first time we were all together was at Will's birthday — we met at a hibachi grill in Parkland. Everyone was polite but no one made eye contact with Tom. He held a very smug attitude and acted as if nothing had ever happened. I was so worried about how the dinner would play out, I could feel the heat rising from my neck up through my face. My family didn't rock the boat — they wouldn't want to do or say anything that would jeopardize our well-being. I can only imagine how distressing it was for them to be around Tom after everything he put all of us through during the past nine months.

I was open with Tom that he would have to earn back my trust. He did take a urine test, although he went into the bathroom and closed the door. He came out with the test showing a negative result for everything including opioids. Who knows, he could have smuggled in clean pee? He went back to pill popping during the course of our reconciliation. He was totally full of shit. Whatever it was, that analysis came back clean. He was very dramatic about all of it. He bought a lock box for the pills and said I could distribute them to him. It was a lock with a key. Maybe he had a duplicate key? All I know is he definitely continued to pop pain pills, even if he was hiding it.

Of all shows we binged on during the reconciliation period, one was the series *Dexter*. It was about a serial killer, psychopath, without a heart. He focused his homicidal desires on the bad guys. But it was Dexter's description of his inner life, his lack of emotion, his mask, that struck me. The eerie thing was that while Tom and I watched the series together, I would comment to him that he was like Dexter. I don't even know why I said it. But something in me saw it. Saw the psychopath. I was making connections and seeing parallels between the character Dexter and my husband who was sitting next to me on the couch.

Even stranger was that Tom didn't deny it. He chuckled when I made the comparison between them. Listen, if someone said that to me, that I was like Dexter, I'd be like, "What the hell are you talking about?!" But Tom's reactions, or lack of reactions, were bizarre. It was ominous considering the actions that eventually took place, that during our reconciliation, we binged on *Dexter*. It was eight seasons — it was a long binge.

We drank wine together in the evenings. He always poured it and made sure my glass was never empty. The next morning I would become violently ill. I didn't have a strong stomach when it came to alcohol, but that was different. I drank alcohol socially, long enough to know what a hangover felt like. I had pounding headaches, my stomach was in shreds and I couldn't function. I was projectile vomiting nightly. I was in bed a lot. He did all the cooking. He poured all the drinks. Will also was sick more often than not during the time we attempted to reconcile. I had every reason to believe he was lacing our food and drinks with something. I had never been that sick before. It sounds outrageous but we may never really know the extent that Tom went through to bring harm to us.

Chapter 30
The Point Of No
Return

One night, Will wasn't feeling well and was having trouble going to sleep. He didn't have a fever, so I didn't give him Tylenol or Motrin. That night I stayed with him in his room. I snuggled him, stroking his arms and his back to comfort him. We were in the dark. I was trying to keep stimulation to a minimum, but he couldn't fall asleep. I was exhausted. Around 2 a.m. I went to wake up Tom and asked him to lay with William for a little while because I had to go to work the next morning. He agreed.

I asked him to wake me up a few hours later. I went back to my room after kissing Will and I fell asleep for a couple hours. I woke up and looked at the clock and it was 4 a.m. I could hear Will's voice, he was still awake.

I went into his room and when I turned on the light to see what was going on, I didn't understand. William sat up in his bed and then proceeded to vomit. I thought, oh that's probably why he wasn't able to sleep, he had an upset stomach. I encouraged him to get down off the bed so I could help to clean him up. When his feet hit the floor he stumbled. He was swaying and reached out in front of him with his hand like he was trying to touch something. His eyes were glazed. I'd never seen him like that.

I looked at Tom and said, "What did you give him?"

He said nothing.

I didn't let up. "What did you give him?"

"Oh I gave him Motrin. I thought it would help him sleep."

"Motrin is for a fever. How much did you give him?" I asked.

He motioned to a capful, which is way more than a toddler needs.

I immediately knew something was wrong and asked him to call 911. He tried to argue with me and said that Will was fine. I screamed at him to call 911. He did and was put through to poison control. I remember him talking to poison control and telling them he gave William too much Motrin. That call triggered a response from the paramedics but it also triggered Broward Sheriff Office in Parkland — my house had been flagged because of the previous domestic violence incident. So when the 911 call came in about our child, the sheriff was sent to our house as well.

I remember the sheriff looking at me. Not in an intimidating way. In an "I want to help you" way. I read it in his face and his body language.

The paramedics came into Will's room and I explained his symptoms and how he was behaving. They looked into his eyes and continued looking him over, but then started to say that they thought if it was Motrin, he would be okay and didn't need to go to the hospital.

Then the sheriff spoke up. "I think to be safe, he should go to the hospital."

I agreed. I never saw him acting like that and I knew I would feel better if he went in. So I got in the ambulance with William and Tom followed us. When we got to the hospital, they started an IV and ran blood tests to see if any drugs were in his system, but they came back clear.

I wish I would have asked if they checked for Ambien. Now I know how people act when they are on it and awake. I can bet with every fiber in my being Tom could have given William Ambien to get him to go to sleep. He's not above doing that and using his own child as a guinea pig to see if it would work.

The hospital staff was preparing to release us. While I was sitting in the room with Will and Tom, the sheriff was standing by the nurse's station and he caught my eye. He signaled with his finger for me to come over to him.

Tom saw me move to get up and he looked over and saw the sheriff.

"He wants to talk to me," I said, and shrugged my shoulders.

I went over and the sheriff asked me in a low voice, under his breath, "Is everything alright at home?"

Without skipping a beat, without even really thinking, I answered honestly.

"No."

He said, "Ok, here's what's going to happen. You're going to be released and I will meet you at your house. There will be a Child Protective Services investigator that will also meet us there. We're going to get you out of this." As he finished those words, Tom sauntered over.

The sheriff completely deflected and asked how Will was doing. It was a relief. Everything seemed surreal. When we were discharged,

I knew what was going to happen. But when I got in the car with Will and Tom, I had to pretend I knew nothing.

Tom immediately started in on me when we left. He said, raising his voice at me angrily, "You know, we can get into trouble for this. You know that. I can get in trouble for this. You overreacted." I played it off that everything was alright and not a big deal. He continued saying there was no reason to call 911, that they could take Will from us.

I played calm and cool. We got to the house. A few minutes later, the sheriff and female investigator from Child Protective Services knocked on the door.

She was our guardian angel — she saved us.

The sheriff stayed in the kitchen with Tom and she pulled me aside into the hallway where Tom couldn't see or hear me.

And she went hard on me.

"Here's what you need to do," she said. "You're going to pack a bag for yourself and a bag for your son. You're going to get into your car, you're going to go to your parents' house. You are leaving him. You are not going back to him. If I find out you're back with him, I'm taking your son."

I didn't even hesitate. I threw my hands up, that was all I needed to hear. "I'm outta here," I said, and thanked her. I asked if they were going to talk to Tom and she said yes.

I didn't look at him. I walked past him, went into the bedroom, and packed my bag and a bag for Will. I put my cat in the carrier, packed up the car and left. To my knowledge they stayed behind and talked to him. I went over to my parents' house and filled them in.

That was the last time. I never went back again or entertained the thought. I was done with him.

Chapter 31
Dependency Court

The State of Florida brought charges against Tom and the case went to Dependency Court. In the Broward County Courthouse, Dependency Court is where charges are brought against a parent, on behalf of a child. When Tom drugged William and we went to the hospital, child protective services became involved.

Tom supposedly left Florida and went back up to the D.C. area, after he drugged Will — and after I left him again. Throughout the nine months the case was open, Tom was supposed to complete a rehabilitation program. It was stupid. It consisted of bullshit parenting classes and anger management. There was a list of 10 things he was required to do over the nine months.

He would fly down once a month and have a supervised — never overnight, visit with William. He hired a female supervisor, whom he, of course, snowed and manipulated. She was completely on his side. They would do things like not respond to texts and show up early to pick him up from preschool. The school knew what was going on, they knew they couldn't release him until a certain time. But he and the supervisor would show up and create discomfort for everyone. Then they'd be late to drop him off and I would worry. My dad and I actually sat down and talked with the supervisor to explain the history and what had been going on.

She didn't believe us.

We warned her that she was dealing with a man who was manipulative. Not to be trusted. She responded with how nice he was and that he was in the military. She didn't see that he was a bad person. She chalked it up to him making some bad choices. She thought we were overreacting. It was frustrating. We gave her printouts about the warning signs of a sociopath. I told her about things that he had done leading up to the reason why he was having supervised visits. She placated us and said she'd keep it in mind.

Toward the end of the dependency case, on the second to last of the supervised visits, Tom screwed over the supervisor. He would always meet her at Walmart, a mile or two away from my home. He would pick her up and they would come to the house and pick up William. On that particular visit, he knocked at my door, by himself. I was confused. She was supposed to be with him. He was not allowed to spend time with William unsupervised. I didn't know what to do. I didn't know what legal ramifications would fall on me if I didn't let William go, or if I demanded the supervisor be there. He talked me into it. He said she was late and he was just going to pick her up at Walmart.

I let William go with Tom.

Tom did go to Walmart to pick up the supervisor and she was livid with him. He went against the policy. He didn't care. But the light bulb went off for her. She contacted me after that visit and apologized. She said she finally understood what I was talking about. It was only because he fucked with her though. That was the only reason why she believed that there was something off with Tom.

There were two more unsupervised visits. Tom joined the American Legion, in the next town over in Margate, Florida. Apparently, he met an elderly woman whom he won over. She had rented him an upstairs room in her home. It was a weird situation. The unsupervised visits were there and one time I had to drop Will off there. Tom was constantly texting me the entire time he was with William. He was obsessed with me. One time I asked him why he was incessantly texting me. "Why don't you spend time with your son? That is what you want. Why are you spending your time texting me?"

Everything about him was bizarre. And creepy.

Chapter 32
No Boundaries

Late one night in January, after I left for good — Tom came onto my parents' property and vandalized my car and my dad's car, both of which were in the driveway. During the reconciliation time frame, we had fixed a dent on the side of my car, replaced the windshield wipers and a few other things. Tom put a new dent in the same place and took the windshield wipers off. He also cut the cable to the a/c underneath the car, *and* let the air out of all four tires. In addition, he slashed a tire on my dad's car. We called BSO and explained what was going on with my ex. They fingerprinted my car but ultimately were unable to identify anything and we couldn't prove it was him.

I confronted him via text. Of course, he denied having anything to do with it and laughed at me. He literally mocked me.

And he didn't stop there.

When we talked of reconciling, Tom enticed me with his military pension, disability payments plus a new six-figure job. He said that we no longer needed my income and I could stay home with Will. I trusted and believed him.

And I quit my job.

I told my manager an elaborate made-up story about why I was resigning because I was too embarrassed to tell her I was getting back with Tom. She was aware of all the crazy events leading up to the reconciliation. She had stuck by me and supported me through all of it. But that wasn't enough to stop me from going back to Tom. I claimed I had a new job — what I did was ridiculous and it took me a long time to overcome the shame. I compromised my integrity for him.

Tom made the situation even worse. After I left him and never returned, he retaliated. He hacked into my Gmail account, and emailed my manager as if he was ME. He rambled on as if I was crazy and drunk, saying I lied to her. She was livid. When I saw her response, my stomach dropped. I scrambled to explain.

But she was done. She had enough. There was no redemption after that. I do not blame her at all.

Then the pressure was on to find a new job. I was hired in a marketing position for a dental insurance company starting in December 2011. Then in January 2012, after I had only been there a month, Tom vandalized my car. I had to disclose to my new manager what was going on. I was hoping to start fresh, without any drama. Fortunately, my manager saved me in many ways. I can't thank her, the company and the COO enough. They continued to have my back for four years.

I was much more fortunate with the support of my employer than so many women in my situation. I'm forever thankful.

Nothing was off limits to Tom.

Chapter 33
Court System
Failings

When Child Protective Services (CPS) gave me the ultimatum to leave Tom, or lose my son — I left for good. It was November 2011. Tom continued to live in the marital home and I stayed with William at my parents' house. From November to January, he constantly harassed me via text and email. In all of his communication attempts to reel me back in, he downplayed what happened when he gave William medication, or used gaslighting to try to confuse me. Part of the deal we made when we reconciled was that his lawyer would prepare a voluntary withdrawal of the restraining order and I would sign it. Tom was adamant there be a clause in the document that said he could retrieve his guns, however he never went back to pick them up.

Tom was angry that the State of Florida, through CPS, decided to bring charges against him for what he'd done to William. In retrospect, it is interesting that the state did follow through with charges because the toxicology report came back clean. They were going on the history of domestic violence and my word.

We were assigned a CPS manager for his case plan. She met with my parents, William and me, to explain the process. She would visit us every month for the duration of the investigation, take pictures of William, check his bedroom to make sure he had a bed to sleep on, and verify there was food in the fridge. What? William's life with *me* would be under scrutiny?

I felt violated. I was not the offending parent, there were no charges against me! Tom was the one who had supervised visitation with William! It was protocol, but it still felt like my parenting was being watched. I'd done nothing!

The plan, overseen by Dependency Court, lasted from December 2011 to September 2012. But in January — after vandalizing our cars — Tom decided to bail from the area again. Supposedly he was heading back to the D.C. area, although I'll never know if that's what he did or just remained in Florida, in hiding.

There was a lot I didn't know about him.

There were ten steps Tom was required to complete to gain back unsupervised visits with William. They tracked him and his case plan progress. There were anger management classes, parenting classes, random drug testing, along with several more steps he had to complete before he could see William without a supervisor.

His attorney was always arguing about the process, saying that Tom did an online class although he was supposed to be physically present at the class in Florida. They dragged their feet on every step, and he never actually completed all the steps. During that time we would have to go to court every few months in front of a magistrate. I didn't even have to be there, but I always went, to be present as William's mother. That magistrate was awful. She treated me the same way she treated Tom even though the charges were against him. I felt as if she thought I was responsible and she blamed me just as much. It felt horrible and degrading.

In the dependency case, Tom had his slime bag divorce attorney representing him. This guy reminded me of some '70s lounge lizard. Out-of-date cheap suits, thinning feathered hair, no scruples at all. There also was a lawyer from the state, a guardian ad litem who was an attorney to act in William's best interests, and a woman hired by the guardian ad litem to come regularly to my home so she could check in on us. This was in addition to the CPS manager. No one checked up on Tom's living circumstances.

When Tom was allowed supervised visits with William, they asked *me* to supervise them. I'm not sure who's crazy, twisted idea that was but I flat out said no, I couldn't supervise his visits. Then they asked if one of my parents could do it. I informed them that we were not going to put ourselves in that kind of position, absolutely not.

Later that summer, the CPS manager was getting anxious to close our case. Apparently, they like to have them wrapped up within nine months. They don't want cases lingering longer than that. She told me they were dropping the random drug testing because he had prescriptions for the drugs he was taking and that's what the tests were showing. He was testing positive for opioids. I said, "Well yeah, he has prescriptions for them, but he's crushing them and he's as high as a kite driving around with our child." It didn't matter. They excused it from the case plan. Then they let a couple other things slide as well. They accepted his online anger management and parenting classes, even though they were supposed to be taken in person.

The last time I met with the CPS manager, she asked me if I thought Tom was a danger to William, and I said I wasn't sure that he would directly hurt William, but definitely I was his target. He was a danger to me, and William was with me all of the time, so by default, my child was in danger.

They didn't take that into account either. They wanted to close the case.

In the meantime, I went three different times to the courthouse to ask for restraining orders. The judge who issued the first temporary restraining order denied all three subsequent orders. The investigator from CPS, who gave me the ultimatum to leave Tom, also requested that I file a restraining order for myself and one for William. She believed it would be granted, but it was not. She was shocked. I went another time after that to apply again, and it was denied as well. The judge said I didn't have enough evidence that Tom was a threat!

Throughout his Dependency Court program, Tom continued to text and harass me. He threatened that as soon as the case was over, he was filing for at least 50/50 custody. He told me he would win and I knew Florida sided with fathers for 50/50 custody. Because Tom had more money, and was retired while I was working, he'd be perceived as the better parent. I didn't put up with his bullshit. I challenged him, but I knew it was going to be a difficult fight — as everything with him was difficult.

When we had the final hearing for the dependency case, on September 25, 2012, we didn't have a Family Court judge assigned yet. We had no visitation order. I begged the dependency court magistrate to set a court-ordered short term visitation schedule that we could abide by until we got in front of a judge weeks or months later. She dismissed me, saying, "No, that's a Family Court thing." I cried.

Then the magistrate said, *"I feel bad for that child having the two of you for parents."* My mouth dropped open.

Then she closed the case.

When the hearing ended I found myself standing in the hallway with my attorney, Tom and his slime bag attorney, negotiating a verbal agreement for visitation.

Nothing was legally enforceable.

Chapter 34
Co-Parenting
Nightmares

We had nothing in writing and I was terrified when we left the courthouse with only a verbal agreement. I didn't have a lawyer for the Family Court case. I needed one fast. I had a conversation with a woman I worked with and she referred me to a lawyer who'd worked wonders for her friend in a contentious divorce like mine.

I met with that lawyer and gave her the background of what happened with my case. She was another guardian angel for us. She worked with us financially — as we'd already dumped so much money into my first attorney, with nothing to show for it — and

146 • KILLING KATE

agreed that we could make monthly payments. I hired her right away. She got the ball rolling to get us in front of a Family Court judge.

According to the verbal agreement made in the hallway, Tom was going to have every other weekend, and a couple dinners per week. The first weekend he had William, Tom said he was going to take him on a cruise. I pleaded with him, saying, "Listen you've been out of his life for a long time. He doesn't even know you that well. Please just stay local." I think he was trying to fuck with me. He was trying to scare me. "William is 3 years old, you need to start slow with him."

"Ok, I'll take him to Disney World," Tom said.

And there was not a thing I could do about it.

Off they went, although I have no proof if they actually went to Disney, or if it was a tactic to scare me. He kept texting me throughout their time together and sending me pictures of William. One was on a bus. I couldn't tell where they were. He made sure I didn't know exactly where they were. Tom tortured me that whole weekend. He texted that he was really drunk the first night. On the second night, he told me he had a date and was getting a babysitter for Will. I said, "You're at Disney with your son. What do you mean you're going on a date and getting some stranger to watch our son?" He had just begun having unsupervised visits and that was how he chose to spend his time with William?

"Yeah, it'll be fine," Tom replied. He laughed at me. Then he texted a picture of William looking terrified. He was holding a bag of candy, his eyes looked glazed and his smile forced through gritted teeth. He looked like a child hostage. I felt paralyzed with fear. My mother screamed when I showed it to her and she asked me to call the police. "We know how this goes, Mom," I said. "I don't have a court order. There is nothing we can do." It was the most helpless moment of my life. There was nothing I could do to protect my child from that monster.

By Sunday I was a basket case. I hadn't slept. I was hoping for texts. As long as I could hear from him, I could assume things were ok. I had no idea if he would return with William at 6 p.m. that evening as we agreed. I was facing the fact that the courts failed me. The parenting time was diminished to a verbal agreement.

Thankfully, he did show up with William. It was the biggest relief to have my baby back in my arms. No mother should ever have to feel that fear. Or feel that level of helplessness. Or know that there is no one to turn to who can help.

It was a failure of the system, a failure of society, that those events even happened.

The emotional abuse continued from September into October via threatening custody, texting and emailing me constantly, and harassing me about being a family — putting that all behind us for Will. The man terrified me. I feared what he was capable of. I knew to keep the boundary. I also knew I didn't want to fight back with him anymore. Naively, I thought that he was a coward, that he wouldn't actually attack me because he would fear going to jail so much more. "He's so OCD," I thought. "He bleaches everything. He couldn't handle being in jail with men who would kick his ass. He loves to bully women and children, not men."

Chapter 35
Birthday Havoc

We hadn't made any payments on the house in nine months. I was living there but it was going into foreclosure and I had plans to move. Tom told me he was going to make payments again and move in. Either that or he'd sell it and I wasn't going to get a dime. I was represented by a lawyer again, so I knew that could be dealt with.

My 40th birthday was approaching, October 22, 2012. I decided to throw myself a '80s themed birthday party. I had been through so much and thought I could use some enjoyment. My plan was to move into my new apartment a week before my birthday, move the furniture I bought with the credit cards in my name, and then have the party in the empty marital home. We would have a lot of room.

We could party and trash it if we wanted to and leave. Then turn the house over to him.

So that was exactly what I did. I had my birthday party on Saturday, October 20 surrounded by my newer Florida friends, friends from work, and some of my childhood and college friends. I had lots of family there, too, including my parents. A guy I worked with was a wedding DJ who said he would DJ my party at no cost. He came with all his equipment. The living room was empty so we had a dance floor. We had food and a keg of beer, lots of wine and liquor. We danced and sang, partied hard, and had the best time.

I was not going back to clean up. He could go fuck himself. My cousin was dancing with red wine in her hand and it splattered on the wall. There was beer on the floor and some food too. It smelled like a frat house afterwards — and we left it that way.

It felt really, really good to do that.

I had to turn the keys over for the marital home to Tom two days later, my 40th birthday. That was the day Tom began visitations with William, after Dependency Court. I could have fought for no visitation that day, but I was worn down. We also lacked an official visitation schedule signed by a judge. Our situation had peaked with uncertainty. I never knew what to expect. I didn't want to take a chance of not letting Will go with Tom because it was my birthday and we had plans. I was trying not to rock the boat more than it already was. I was trying to keep the peace and hold everything together, with the intention that he would behave less crazily.

During that day of his scheduled visit, we were to meet at the marital home at 6 p.m. Tom would drop off William to me and I'd to go to my parents' house for a birthday celebration. I was going to give him the keys to the marital home because he said that he was going to take over the house. I didn't want it, nor could I afford it.

He started fucking with me in the early afternoon, saying they were going to be late for our scheduled drop off. "I'm going to be late. I won't be there by 6," he threatened. I asked him not to do that, it was my birthday and I had dinner plans with my family. "Well I'm gonna be even more late," he told me. "I don't know what time I'm going to be able to get there." I asked what he was planning. He had the "read receipt" function enabled, so I knew he read the text but didn't respond to me. And then he sent a text a little bit later saying, "I'm not sure what time." He was torturing me throughout the day. I told him if he wasn't there by 6 p.m., I was going to call the police. He said, "Go ahead. There's nothing the police can do anyway."

I arrived at the marital home and went inside to wait. Six o'clock came and went. I texted him and asked if he was almost at the house. I could see the "read receipt" but again no response from him. "How much longer do you think you'll be?" Read receipt and no response. "I'm calling the police, I don't know where you are, I'm receiving no response from you and it's time for you to return William." I called Parkland BSO and got a couple different deputies that I had never met before. They shrugged it off. There wasn't much they could do, they informed me. I didn't have a restraining order and I didn't have a parenting-time order signed by the judge. One of them even said he could be halfway to Canada and there was really nothing they could do. I burst into tears, I felt helpless. This guy was determined to do whatever he wanted to at any expense.

I called my dad to ask him to come over and wait with me. I was a nervous wreck. The police were still there when Tom drove around the corner. He pulled up and got out of the car and said, "Is there something wrong officers?" Then he turned his gaze to me with the most smug, asshole face that spoke directly to me — it's a game and he's going to win.

The officers told Tom I was concerned and he had no response. In the meantime, my dad went over to the car to get William. I was standing near the car, with my arms crossed, glaring at Tom. I mouthed "fuck you." His expression changed from smug to dark and evil. As they say, if looks could kill, he would have.

My brother, sister-in-law and their kids were at my parents' house waiting and the next thing I knew, my brother was driving up. My brother was furious. He had never confronted Tom before. It was hard for my family to know what to do to help me. But my brother had enough. He put his car in park in the middle of the road, got out, and in front of the police officers yelled, "You're a fucking piece of shit, get out of the car, I'm going to beat your ass!"

The smug look returned to Tom's face, as if he enjoyed the scene. The officers diffused the situation and told my brother that they didn't want to have to arrest him. They asked him to get back into his car, followed by, "If he drives away and you follow him, there's really nothing we can do about that…"

And that's what happened. When they drove away, my dad, William and I went back to my parents' house. After a while my brother came back, hyped up. He had followed Tom a mile from our marital home to the Walmart parking lot. My brother drove next to him, mocking him. Tom went into the Walmart parking lot and put his car in park. My brother put his car in park and started to get out. Tom was walking towards Matt and Matt baited Tom, "Come on fucker, hit me! Hit me!" Tom turned around and got back in his car. Matt could see he was on his phone, and assumed he was calling the police. Matt drove off and returned to my parents' house, out of breath and fired up, telling us what had happened.

We'd so wished Tom had thrown that first punch. My brother would have kicked his sorry ass from there to Australia.

But that was yet another example of a typical abuser. Tom was scary and threatening to women and children until another man confronted him — then he cowered.

Chapter 36
The Final Straw

The next day, October 23, while at work, I got a call from the CPS investigator, our guardian angel. She said, "Kate, Tom called in a child abuse report on you, saying that Will has bruises on his legs. I know what we're dealing with here, but because he called something in, I have to come over and check William. Can you pick him up from school and meet me at your parents' house?" Had it been *any* other investigator, who knows what would have happened with a false child abuse allegation. Again it was another situation where she saved us by interception. I don't know how to explain why and how it happened the way it did, but we were so very fortunate that this woman saw who Tom was.

I had to inform my manager about what was going on. How embarrassing! To this day, I cannot believe I had to bring this level of personal drama into my work life. Had I worked for any other manager or any other company, I'm sure I would've been fired.

I left work to pick up Will and go over to my parents' house. The investigator and a female BSO deputy arrived to look over William's legs and of course concluded he was fine. She asked what was going on between Tom and I, were things escalating? I told her that Tom would leave for the weekend with Will, not tell me where he was and constantly texted me. He consistently dropped Will off late, and demanded more and more time with him in a threatening way.

I also mentioned I had no visitation order signed by a judge.

"Whoa," she said and then asked, "When Dependency Court closed, did it end with you having full physical custody, including decision making?"

Yes it did.

"You don't have to turn William over, Kate," she informed me. "He's not seeing Tom until there's a visitation order signed by a judge. You are not to give him over again."

I asked her if she was going to break the news to Tom and she said she would.

I felt so relieved. And I had an official behind me, someone to turn to who had instructed me on this. I informed my attorney of the conversation and she told me she would connect with Tom's attorney and request a negotiation about custody and parenting time. She said she told Tom's attorney, "The sooner we get a visitation schedule in place, the sooner your client can see his son again."

Our CPS investigator confirmed that she'd had the conversation with Tom.

Then it became very quiet. He stopped emailing me. He stopped texting me. Tom's lawyer didn't respond to my lawyer.

Chapter 37
Silence Before
The Storm

For ten days there was silence.

It was twofold. On one hand, it felt odd since he had been constantly harassing me, threatening custody. On the other hand, it felt glorious. I began to enjoy my life with the reprieve.

I also knew that Tom knew he was losing. His child abuse report was deemed bullshit. He couldn't see William anymore until we had a court order. I also figured he was likely pissed off at the state of our home when he went in after getting the keys back. He lost all the control he once had. This was a guy who had skated through life and gotten away with everything up until that point. He was experiencing women telling him what he could not do. Not only me but also an African American female. He thought he was above both of us.

Then it was Friday November 2, 2012.

I'd worked, just like any normal Friday. I was dating a coworker. We had plans to go out to dinner that evening. After work, I picked up William from preschool, about a mile from my new apartment. I took a selfie with William when we got home. It's ominous and a little creepy to look at now. My eyes spoke of fear and William had a very serious expression, he wasn't smiling at all. I changed my clothes and began making Will a snack while he was watching TV. It was nearing the time to go to dinner. My dear friend Tanya and her daughters, who lived next door to my parents, were going to watch Will. I got Will ready, we went out to the car and I buckled him in. I got into the driver's seat, turned the car on and some of the light indicators flashed on the dashboard. One said "low tire pressure."

Immediately, my mind raced. "Oh shit, he found me." I'd moved into my new apartment and not given him the address. But when he vandalized my car previously at my parent's home, it was the same experience. The lights came on and said "low tire pressure" because he'd let the air out of my tires.

I instinctively knew. I knew it was him.

I got out of the car, looked at the tires on my side and didn't see anything. I walked around to look at the passenger side and there was a large slash in the front tire. It appeared sliced right through with a knife.

Fuck.

I got William out of the car and took him inside. I was pissed. He fucking found me. How did he find me? I never gave him my address.

I called my dad and he said he would come over. He told me to call the police in the meantime. I called my boyfriend too — he was aware of everything that was going on with Tom. I told him what happened. He said he would cancel dinner and I suggested we go over to my parents' house and hang out so we could figure out a plan for what to do next.

My dad arrived first and he waited in the apartment with Will when I saw the police car pull up. I met the female officer in the parking lot and showed her the tire. I explained the history of our situation in a nutshell.

The first question she asked was if I had a restraining order.

I said I didn't. She said there was nothing she could do without seeing a restraining order. There was no way to prove it was Tom who slashed the tire. "What you can do is go to the Domestic Violence Division at the courthouse, it is open on Saturday," she said. "You can go tomorrow and file for a restraining order."

"I've been turned down *three times* by the same judge so I don't know what good that will do," I said.

"There's really nothing I can do right now without a restraining order."

Before she turned to leave, I said to her, *"HE'S GOING TO HAVE TO KILL ME BEFORE YOU PEOPLE DO ANYTHING TO STOP HIM."*

She walked away.

I was so pissed. I felt defeated. I felt helpless. I thought "fuck the system."

In fact, even before I called the police, I knew there was nothing they would do. I'd been through it enough to know that without the order, they couldn't do anything. She didn't even ask for a description or to see a picture of him, or ask about his car, or look around the premises. Nothing.

I went back into the house and my dad suggested I call roadside assistance to come and change the tire. William and I could go to their house and together we could make a plan for the next steps. I agreed.

My dad opened the door to leave and walked partway down the sidewalk. Then he turned back towards me and said, "Katie, call 911. Tom is here."

I looked into the parking lot and I saw the dome light inside his car. I saw him start to get out of the car. I immediately dialed 911. My dad told me to go inside and he would stay outside with Tom. I was not comfortable with that, my dad having to deal with him.

My gut was screaming at me.

"No Dad, come inside with me," I said. Whatever Tom was there for, I didn't want to leave my dad alone outside with him. He listened.

Then both of us were inside the apartment.

Chapter 38
I Told You So

It happened mind-blowingly fast. Ambush style. No time to think.

Tom started pushing on the front door to my apartment to force his way in. I was on the phone with 911.

In the recording of the 911 call, they could hear me say, "My estranged husband is here and he's trying to force himself into the home."

My dad and I were pushing on the door from the inside to keep Tom out. We were facing the front door, pushing as hard as we could with both hands. I was on the left, dad was on the right near the door handle. Dad was trying to lock it and he could see the side of Tom's face.

Little William, who was 4-years-old, was standing just behind us.

"I just want to talk to Kate. I just want to talk to Kate. I just want to talk to Kate," Tom kept repeating.

Then BANG! BANG! BANG!

Bullets came blasting through the door. We didn't even know he had a gun.

It was animalistic screaming I heard coming from my mouth. A sound I'd never before heard myself make.

I backed up to the kitchen table. My dad went the other way toward the couch and William was standing in the middle.

Tom entered with the gun drawn — and he pointed it at me.

BANG!

My right hand exploded in front of my face.

I never felt pain like that before. My hand went limp. It was dangling. I couldn't move it. I fell to the ground but as I did, my hand went behind me and blood splattered up the wall. I knew I was in trouble.

I hit the ground. Terrorized, I screamed at the top of my lungs, begging him not to do it, not to shoot again.

"Why did you take my stuff?" he yelled. "Why did you take my stuff? Why did you take my military stuff? Was it worth it, you fucking bitch?"

He screamed none of that cliché shit other men say when they've done bad things to a woman like, "I miss my son," or "I just want us to be a family," or "If I can't have you, no one will."

No, he was yelling about the belongings I'd taken from the house to my new apartment — the things I'd put on *my* credit cards.

As for the "military stuff," I still don't know what he was talking about.

I was begging, screaming and apologizing for taking the stuff anyway. "I'll give it back to you!" I pleaded.

Anything to get him not to shoot me in the head. Because that's what I was waiting for.

"Tom, please, please. I'm sorry, I'm so sorry," I begged. "I'll return it. I'll give everything back. Don't do this."

Tom looked at me. He was drunk with power. "I killed your brother Kate, he took my fucking mountain bike."

"Nooooooo!" I screamed. I couldn't take it. He looked smug. He was enjoying torturing me.

At one point he turned and went over to my father who was on the ground. My dad knew he had been shot and was attempting to call 911 from his cell phone. Tom ordered him to drop his phone and to push it away.

Then I heard BANG! Then I heard a grunt.

Again, I screamed, "Nooooooo!"

Tom came back towards me again. I managed to crawl farther away from him. I was sliding on the floor in my own blood. I was completely covered in my blood. I could smell it. My hair was slick and sticking to my head. My clothes clung to me. I felt limp and my hand was throbbing.

I laid there, looking between the table and chair legs. He used a 9mm Beretta to shoot us, one with a red laser on it. He was shining the laser at me between the table and the legs on the chair, taunting me with every move.

William was on the other side of the table, in the middle of the room. After Tom shot my dad, he went over and knelt down next to Will.

It was quiet for a moment.

And then: "Don't do it, Daddy! Don't shoot Mommy!"

William, my 4-year-old son found the words.

There was silence again.

I was waiting for the police to come and kick the door in. But it didn't happen like it should have. It wasn't like in the movies or on TV. A SWAT team didn't kick the door in, and kill the bad guy.

It seemed as though I was lying there in my blood for a very long time. It seemed that no one was coming to help us. He was pointing the laser at me. I was waiting for the shot that would kill me.

The Killing Kate shot.

Then Tom said, "Kate, there's a table runner on the table. Grab it and wrap the wound."

I was robotic. Without thinking, I grabbed it and wrapped it around my hand.

Then he said, "Just go. Just go."

Those words weren't said with a hint of remorse. He knew the cops were outside. He was just playing the odds. And he knew I was gravely wounded.

"Yeah right," I thought. "He's just going to shoot me when I leave." I also knew I wasn't doing well — if I stayed, I'd die right there on my floor.

So I took my chance.

I got up, staggered through the front door, took a few steps onto the grass and my legs turned to liquid. I collapsed.

"Katherine, can you get over here to us?" the police called out.

What the hell? They couldn't come over to help me? With their bullet-proof vests?

My dad came out next with William in front of him.

HE WAS ALIVE!

Tom told my dad to leave too and my dad picked himself up off the floor. He told William, "It's time to go." He walked hunched down over Will, ready to take a bullet to protect him.

When my dad was leaving, Tom said, "She's gone."

My dad thought that I was dead. He didn't know that I had walked out the front door. I thought he was dead after I heard Tom take the second shot.

I thought my father was dead — my father thought I was dead. Let that sink in.

"Sir, can you grab her and bring her over to us?" the police called out.

My dad bent down near me and grabbed my arm with a strength I never felt from him before.

"Come on, Katie, you gotta get up, we gotta go," my dad said. I had nothing left. With the table runner still wrapped around my hand, I lifted myself up to my feet with stamina that was not my own. My dad was a hero. He got my son and me.

We laid down behind the cars to wait for medical assistance.

And then I saw her. It was the second time we met that day. Only then the officer was hovering over me. "I'm sorry, I'm sorry, I'm so so sorry!" she cried.

With uninhibited primal screams, like they were coming from someone else, someone who didn't have life draining out of her, I roared, "I FUCKING TOLD YOU! I FUCKING TOLD YOU HE WAS GOING TO DO THIS TO ME!"

I didn't lose consciousness but I was unaware of what everyone was doing around me. My dad and I were lying on the grass. An officer scooped up Will and took him far away from the scene for safety.

My dad was screaming in a carnal reaction I'd never heard before. He was bellowing, "Katie, Katie, Katie!" over and over. He thought he was going to lose me. He noticed in addition to my hand, I was bleeding from my chest too.

I ALSO TOOK A BULLET IN MY LEFT BREAST.

The police department was ridiculous. Even in my own precarious state, I could tell they had no idea what to do next. My dad was telling them to put pressure on my chest wound, to take off his shirt and use it for that purpose.

My clothes were sticking to me. They cut them off completely.

My boyfriend was standing over me, telling me to look at him, to stay awake. He came onto the scene just after the shooting and before the police arrived. He heard me screaming. He got out of his car and went to the door of the apartment and pushed the door open. Tom turned and pointed the gun at him and shook his head no.

The police arrived when my boyfriend was at the door, and yelled for him to get away from there. He said he couldn't see me. He saw Will crying, and he saw Tom. That was it, he didn't see my dad either. Then he had to leave and wait with the police.

When I came out and fell to the ground, he was yelling at the police to go get me.

Their response was that there was an active shooter, and according to protocol, they couldn't come to get me.

Then there were whispers of a helicopter. The police were that concerned with my condition, with my chest wound. They thought my dad and I both needed to go to a trauma unit at North Broward

Health Center. Dad was going in an ambulance but I was losing so much blood and in critical condition that I needed a chopper. It seemed to take forever. My dad was screaming at them, "Where's the ambulance? Where's the chopper?"

They seemed to be messing with a chain link fence that was near where we laid. I heard the chain rattling behind me. And talk of not being able to open it. And of ambulances having to wait until the suspect was apprehended and there was no more active shooter.

"WHAT THE FUCK IS TAKING SO LONG???" I screamed in my mind. "I'M DYING!!!" I heard my dad vocally yelling about how long it was taking.

Finally, I clearly remember them putting me on a gurney. I remember the bouncy feeling going over the gravel while being wheeled from the shooting location to the chopper, which had landed in a parking lot around the block. I just couldn't believe that was happening.

I was loaded into the helicopter and we took off. The paramedic next to me was quiet — he didn't say much or try to make conversation with me. I focused on the little red light on the ceiling of the helicopter. I refused to close my eyes. My only option was to stay awake. I never lost consciousness. It was instinct somehow.

We landed and I was wheeled out from the landing pad to the hospital emergency room entrance. All of the sudden I heard my brother. "Kate I'm here!"

I thought Tom killed him!

I screamed his name, "Matt, Matt!"

My mom was saying, "Katie, Katie, we're here."

I screamed over and over again like a child, "Mommy, Mommy, Mommy!" I just screamed it. I hadn't called her Mommy since I was a little girl. But that night, in that moment, that was exactly how I felt. Like a little girl who needed her mommy.

They took me into the trauma unit and my mother told me my father was also there and was alive. The paramedics had wrapped my hand — the only time I actually saw the wound was immediately after Tom shot me.

I remember the gore of it. I remember the bloody flesh, hanging. But I was in shock.

There are pictures of my hand after I had surgery — what I call the Frankenstein version — with three inches worth of thick stitches. Part of me wished there were pictures of the pre-surgery wound. It was part of my journey.

It was something that happened to my body and I have no photographic evidence of the true horror.

Chapter 39
Guilt And Shame

I found out in the trauma unit that my dad was actually able to get through to my mom from the ground once we were safely behind the police outside my apartment. My mom received the awful phone call that her husband and her daughter were both shot. She didn't know where William was, so she called my brother. He was overcome with worry and slid down the wall like spaghetti as he listened to our mom in a panic.

My dad told my mom which hospital we were going to and my brother picked her up. They sped through red lights from Parkland to Pompano Beach to get to the hospital. When they arrived, they could see the chopper landing. My mother and brother didn't know if I was alive or dead. My dad was arriving simultaneously in the ambulance and they were unaware of his fate as well.

My mother stayed with me when they brought me into the trauma unit. I was just screaming and screaming. The staff gave me Dilaudid, a heavy pain medicine, which I couldn't handle. I threw up all over. They were very concerned with my chest wound and I remember an X-ray machine they wheeled in that could take an instant image. I remember them yelling, "Oh my God, it's a flesh wound! There's no bullet in her chest! It's a miracle!" The bullet entered the right side of my left breast and went straight out through the left side.

It nearly missed my heart.

It's crazy to think that if I had been positioned any other way against the door, the bullet would have gone directly into my heart.

My brother and mother were going between my unit and my dad's — we were next to each other. My mom told me my dad was alive and she asked me where William was, but I didn't know. What I found out later was that she called my cell phone and my boyfriend had taken it with him. He was at the police station being questioned, and told my mom they'd taken William to the station, too. William was being questioned by a forensic detective, who did an amazing job with him. It was sick and disgusting to think of my child in that position.

I later saw the recording of the interview. Will was so tiny, sitting on a couch in a small room in the police station. He didn't even have shoes on.

"Is Mommy dead?" he asked.

"I don't know buddy," answered the police officer who was with him. "We've got to wait to find out when the detective comes to talk with you."

My poor baby didn't know if his mommy was dead or alive. Horrifying.

From the time they said it was a flesh wound in the chest to when I was admitted upstairs into a hospital room, my memory was foggy. I did not go to the ICU, however my dad did. The bullet Tom shot point blank into his left side was still in him. They were worried about possible organ puncture and internal bleeding. I received a blood transfusion that night because of the amount of blood I lost. I was on a lot of pain medication and it still hurt so badly. Throbbing, searing pain.

My boyfriend stayed with me and I remember just crying and crying. At one point I screamed, "How will my life ever be normal again??? How will my life ever be the same?"

The other thing that hung in my mind was guilt. Crushing guilt. And shame. I was basically mentally flagellating myself for having met Tom, falling for his bullshit, marrying him and having a child with him. I did to myself what many abused women do — I blamed myself for what happened. My dad could have died. Those bullets could have killed William. I was far less concerned for myself and much more focused on my son, my father, my family.

How could I have allowed that monster into our lives?

My dad came out of the ICU once they removed the bullet. We both had surgery the next morning. Mine was on my right hand and my dad's was on his left arm. I absolutely thought my hand would have to be amputated. I didn't think there was any way that it would be salvageable. But when I met with the surgeon that morning, he was positive that he would be able to put my hand back together. He was a long-time trauma surgeon and had done many surgeries like mine, he assured me.

I remember being wheeled into the operating room, placed on the table, with both my arms stretched out to the sides and secured down. There was a blindingly bright light above me. They put an oxygen mask over my face and instructed me to take a deep breath. I remember hearing voices around me —and then it was lights out.

I don't really remember waking up. I don't remember if my mom was there when I was coming out of recovery. I don't remember being brought back to my room.

But I do remember being told he did it. My surgeon fixed my hand.

I don't have any plates, screws or metal in my hand. He was able to put tendons and ligaments back together in a way that was nothing short of miraculous. I lost my pointer finger and middle finger knuckles. My thumb, pointer and middle fingers are shorter on my right hand than my left, due to bone loss.

But my hand is intact.

I was in the hospital for four days and my dad was in for five. I had many visitors. William came with my mom to see me the day after. He was tentative — he knew I was hurt. He and my nephew, both around the same age, climbed up onto the bed and hugged me. It was emotional to see William again. We were so close to never seeing each other again. He had a flower with him. He and my mom stopped at the gift shop in the hospital and he picked a flower to bring to me.

Once I was discharged, it was far from over. We were living at my parents' house. My mom was the rock and basically put all of us back together. I had a picc line in my arm because I needed antibiotics pumped directly into my body for a week — the doctors were worried about infection from my wounds. My mother is very woozy and doesn't like blood or any of that but that woman locked it down for her husband and daughter. She helped me with the antibiotic injections and helped me clean and wrap my hand. She sat with me when I soaked it in Epsom salts. She dressed my dad's wounds.

My mom is a special person. An Earth Angel, really.

My father and I were both in so much pain. I recall one time shortly after we both got out of the hospital, we were each on separate sides of the couch in the middle of the night. We didn't even speak, it hurt so badly that neither of us could sleep. The pain broke through the medication. I couldn't take Percocet or OxyContin because of my stomach. The most I could tolerate was Vicodin and it didn't ease the pain enough.

I would pace during the night around my parents' dining room table. It always hurt and throbbed more during the night. I would hold my right elbow in my left hand and gently bounce my arm up and down. For some reason the motion helped to move and circulate blood flow and distracted me from the pain. It seemed like my hand was swollen to the size of a baseball glove. My fingers were like sausages. There was just so much pressure. It felt like my hand would explode.

I had regular appointments with the surgeon, at least once a week. My best friend was a nurse and she helped to take care of me. She would answer any concerns and help take care of the wounds. She did the same for my dad. She went with me to many of my appointments with the surgeon and one in particular was to remove the stitches in my palm. As he was pulling the stitches out, I could feel the pull and tug. The stitches sliding against my skin freaked me out. I turned white and was close to passing out. As great of a surgeon as mine was, he really had *no* bedside manner at all. I kept saying that it hurt and he was like, "Oh, you're fine." My friend looked at me and knew I wasn't fine, and said that I needed to lay down. He finished pulling out the stitches as I squeezed her hand.

My dad had several appointments with the doctors who worked on him. He had staples in his left arm and those were removed. He also had stitches. We both had extreme bruising at the gunshot sights. Both sides of my left breast had huge black and blue welts. My dad had massive bruising on his left side where he was shot point blank.

One of the last times I saw my surgeon, about a month or so after the shooting, he told me I needed to start occupational therapy to reactivate movement in my hand again. He was adamant. He told me if I didn't go, my hand would become a claw. I wouldn't have range of motion, and I wouldn't be able to use it. He put the fire under me and referred me to an occupational therapist. I began occupational therapy in early December 2012.

My occupational therapist was another miracle worker.

In the beginning, she made many contraptions to support my forearm and my fingers, which wouldn't bend. She made devices out of plastics that she molded to force my fingers down because they were sticking straight up. We did electrode treatments on my hand to stimulate the nerves to make my fingers close again. At the beginning it hurt and I regularly thought I would pass out. She was so patient and positive, yet she pushed me too and I appreciated that. The appointments were three times a week. My OT and other patients there became like family. Everyone was horrified by my story and in turn gave me so much support.

Working on my hand helped me feel I was proactive in my recovery. It took nine months of OT for my hand to make a fist again. That was considered full range of motion.

To this day, my right hand still doesn't look the same. It's much thicker and swollen than my normal-looking left hand. My thumb and pointer and half of my middle finger remain numb. My thumb is kind of off-set from my hand. The bullet damaged my radial nerve. Nerves repair themselves but it takes a very long time. In almost seven years, I don't notice any improvement. There's still a bony indentation in the middle of the top of my hand where the bullet entered, and a long thin scar down the middle of my palm from surgery. My dexterity hasn't improved much either. I can't feel things and compensate with my left hand for most things. Like most professionals, I use a keyboard for work. I can't type the same anymore. I use my middle and ring fingers on my right hand because I can feel the keys. My thumb and pointer are essentially useless.

I've been around and around about how it could've been much worse. I know that. Of course it could have.

I could be dead.

But that's not what happened — and my hand still isn't what it was before the shooting. My hand should not look and feel like it does. My breast should not have round, bullet-wound scars on it.

All are daily reminders.

Chapter 40
The Snitch

About a month after the shooting, I was on the way to my attorney's office. The divorce was not even close to being final when the shooting took place. There was still a lot of work to do. Miraculously, it was put on fast track after he attempted to murder me.

As I pulled into the parking lot, I received a call from the detective on the case. "We have a development," he told me. "A snitch has come forward." An inmate at the jail with Tom went to the guards saying Tom had made inquiries to hire someone to finish the job.

The job was — to kill me.

I couldn't breathe. I already almost died because of him. He was doing what he could do from behind bars to make it happen. He was going to pay someone to murder me.

The detective delivered the message in a calm way, and assured me they were going to handle it. I wasn't ordered to go into hiding. They were taking steps to see if the guy was credible and if the threat was legitimate. They were going to wire the snitch. He told me to "hang in there," because it could take a while. I understood that, but it was so scary. Because it was a death threat, you'd think they could just go in and wire him and find out right away. But it would take a couple of weeks.

From there, it was grey. It was terror. It was awful. I was traumatized from the shooting a month earlier and experiencing a new trauma. It was continued abuse. From behind bars.

I had already been through so much. It felt like that shit was never going to fucking end with that guy. "As long as he was alive, he was going to keep doing things to torture me," I thought. I was constantly looking over my shoulder after the shooting. Then add in the knowledge that he was likely conspiring to have me killed.

A couple months later, I was informed that the snitch was deemed not credible. The theory is that these guys come forward and make a claim, in exchange for perhaps knocking off a couple years from their sentence. They do receive something in exchange for their information and agreement to comply with a wire setup. To my knowledge, the wire never took place. There was a lot of back and forth between the detective and me about that. It was very frustrating. I knew Tom. I believed the snitch. I had zero doubt that he was talking to inmates about ways to pay somebody who was getting out, to go and finish it. Tom had plenty of money, with his military pension that continued even after the shooting.

We'll never know if he kept trying to find someone to comply, and if there were others who never came forward.

Chapter 41
Restraining Orders Granted

After the shooting, one of the first legal acts we took was to file for permanent restraining orders for myself, my dad and William. I had already been turned down three times by the judge. It was a week to ten days after the shooting when we went to the courthouse with our bandages and braces, and sat on the bench in the hallway near the courtroom. Unexpectedly, we heard the sound of chains rattling. We looked up and it was Tom walking by. I was feeling feisty and had my phone in my hand. I was able to quickly snap a picture of him walking past in his jumpsuit and shackles. It felt satisfying to hear the sound of his chains rattling and see that he was incapacitated. Tom looked directly at me, in an attempt to pierce me with his evil stare.

His face looked smug — which was ironic, given his circumstances. He'd failed at his mission.

We were the champions!

In the hearing, my dad went first, represented by my divorce attorney, and it was a quick process. The judge, without questions, promptly granted him a restraining order and got him out of the courtroom. In an interesting and telling spin, the judge wouldn't see me.

He knew he had blood on his hands and couldn't face me. Coward.

He kept my attorney there and on the spot granted permanent restraining orders for William and me. He wouldn't fucking face me. He wouldn't have me in his courtroom. That guy should *not* be deciding who does and doesn't obtain restraining orders.

"Yeah, thanks for giving me a permanent restraining order *after* I'd already been shot," I thought. Tom was already in jail and he wasn't going to get bond. However, we needed the permanent restraining orders so Tom couldn't make any demands on William or correspond with me or my family in any way.

When we met with our first prosecutor assigned to our case, we would eventually go through four, in the years before trial, I was impressed. She had a no-nonsense approach and she knew what she was doing. In a matter-of-fact and upfront way, she told us that although we were the victims, unfortunately in our lovely judicial system, Tom had more rights than we did. Then they discovered that Tom obtained the best defense attorney in Fort Lauderdale. He had a long-standing reputation in Broward County and Fort Lauderdale. He had high-profile clients and was a high-priced lawyer.

Our prosecutor knew he had a reputation for dragging on similar cases. "It could be four or five years before we go to trial," she informed us. We didn't believe her. We thought there was no way it would take that long given the severity of our case. It felt unfathomable that it would take four or five years for a trial. We were naive.

At the time of the shooting, we still didn't have a Family Court judge in place. The divorce was at a standstill. My attorney, thankfully, was able to get the court to fast track the divorce after the shooting. The judge didn't allow any postponement of the divorce hearing, as had been the case before the shooting. We went to court in January, in front of a Family Court judge that was appointed to us. We had to talk about finances, the house and many more details, which would take a significant amount of time. My lawyer demanded that some actions take place immediately, so I could revert back to my maiden name, change my social security card, and we would have an official divorce order.

The financial and house details had to wait until we resolved the issue of Tom's parental rights. About a week after the shooting, we met with our Child Protective Services investigator, our guardian angel, at her office in Fort Lauderdale. She contacted me within days after my release from the hospital, saying the state was going to move to terminate Tom's rights to William, and we needed to get the ball rolling. We were told the termination of a parent's rights was a highly unlikely procedure and judges were not prone to act on it. She told us even with the shooting, it could still be a stretch for his parental rights to be revoked.

Really? He almost commits murder and could have killed his own son — but his blood is biological so that comes first?

But she and the state were determined and I, of course, was fully on board. I didn't want Tom to have a chance for any demands about our son, or to try to pull any sort of power and control moves from behind bars, just because of biology.

Plus, I didn't want my son to carry that disgusting last name any longer.

We got the paperwork started and then it went to the state's attorney. She, an associate and a representative from CPS were involved, and my family and I all were interviewed. As they put their case together, there was a ton of red tape, and it took many motions, which culminated in a trial in July 2013 — eight months after the shooting.

Tom could have made it simple and just signed off his parental rights without a trial. That was an option presented to him. But as with any psychopath, he was determined to make it as difficult as possible.

The trial was held in Dependency Court, ironically with the same judge who served over the magistrate we encountered earlier — the one who made the comment that she felt bad for our child, having us as parents. It was a shit show. The judge was known for wacky, off-the-wall decisions. For letting people off the hook who perhaps should not be free.

It was not a promising start.

She was routinely late and our trial was scheduled to be one-week long. She kept us waiting for a couple of hours at times. I knew Tom was sitting just over in the next room, shackled, but still in close proximity. To him, it was entertainment, to continue to torture and abuse me through the court system. They couldn't force him to sign off on his rights — the state had to prove an entire case. It was such a waste of time and money and it re-victimized all of us.

Once it got started, the trial was held in the judge's quarters, not in a courtroom. It was a small room with a long table and I was in a confined area with Tom. I was positioned directly behind him, since they didn't want Tom looking at me. The range of emotions I felt was extreme. From numbness, to feeling in a fog, to being triggered, to also feeling happy that Tom was being held accountable. "It should have happened a long time ago," I thought. "It should not have taken attempted murder for this to happen."

On another level, it was also satisfying to go through the trial. They told me I didn't need to be there but why the hell wouldn't I be there? It was for my child. I didn't want to miss any of it and I was cautious, taking note of anything I didn't understand or wanted answered. My divorce attorney went with me, through the whole trial.

The state's attorney assigned to the case was amazing. I had full faith in her. She was prepared.

Part way through the trial, she introduced the video of William being questioned by the forensic detective the night of the shooting. It was one of the most heart wrenching things a mother could see. My bare-footed, towheaded, innocent 4-year-old, being questioned about what he saw. I wasn't angry at the detective. At all. He was absolutely amazing with William. And William did a perfect job.

But the video was probably one of the worst things I'll ever see in my life.

"Something happened at your house tonight, didn't it?" asked the detective.

"Yeah," said William, in a small voice. "My daddy shot my mommy."

"Do you like living with your mommy?"

"Yeah."

"Do you like seeing your daddy?"

"No."

"Are you afraid of your daddy?"

"Yeah. He has a gun."

The questioning seemed to go on forever.

The judge was teary-eyed and the state's attorney was visibly upset. I was choking back tears. But I didn't want to leave the room. I wanted to stay right there.

Actually, the only people not upset in the room were Tom and his lawyer. He was represented by his slime bag divorce attorney again. The two of them sat there without any sign of emotion while viewing William's questioning. At one point, I heard Tom chuckle over something William said. "WHAT THE FUCK ARE YOU FUCKING LAUGHING AT?!?!?!" I screamed at him in my head.

At the end of the trial, each attorney gave closing statements and I thought it would be over. But the judge needed to review all the documents, along with the evidence, and would provide her decision to the attorneys.

So I had to put it aside and wait. More waiting. It felt like an eternity.

It was important to me that Tom's parental rights be terminated. Yes, for the principle of it but also, I didn't want him having the capability of making demands or filing motions to force William to see him somehow. He slipped through so many loops during the history of our relationship that I didn't want him to have any legal rights to William. I didn't trust him.

A few people tried to talk me out of it. In the state of Florida, if a parent's rights are terminated, he or she doesn't have to pay child support. That wasn't a deal breaker for me. William's well-being was more important than receiving child support. To this day, I am so glad I made that decision and Will does not have to associate with Tom or anyone in his family.

With the termination of parental rights, I was able to change Will's birth certificate. His dad is no longer listed on it. I changed his last name to my family name, as well as his social security card. All of those steps gave us a feeling of satisfaction and of taking our power back. After not having control of anything for so long, seeing justice take place in several ways was a gratifying feeling. And, on the other hand, I found it extremely annoying that it took near-death trauma for those things to happen — for us to start seeing that justice.

Why did it take a murder attempt for people to hear me? For the system to finally kick in?

Patriarchy, that's why. And misogyny. And that's a book in itself, *Dissolving Toxic Masculinity*.

Chapter 42
The Aftermath

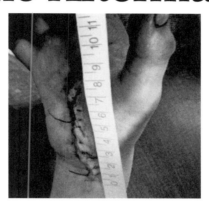

I spent the first eight to nine months after the shooting focused on my physical recovery, going to occupational therapy three times a week. I went back to work after two months. The company I worked for was incredibly supportive — they paid my full salary for two months. That rarely happens in situations like mine. I know too many survivors who've lost their jobs after trauma. I don't know why I didn't take Family Medical Leave after the first two months were up. I probably wasn't thinking clearly. I wish I would have considered that option more.

It was a foggy time. I had bills to pay, my car payment, insurance, etc. Will was in preschool and the parents in his class raised enough tuition to help us for two months. Friends and family cooked and delivered meals to us over several weeks, which was a big help to my mom, who didn't have to think about making dinners.

Unfortunately, I didn't take care of my mental health — not even a little bit. I had been seeing a therapist regularly in the year and one half before the shooting. I loved working with her — she was kind, compassionate and encouraging. I should have been in daily therapy though. I didn't know about post-traumatic stress disorder (PTSD). I put my focus on my physical recovery, on William, and on getting back into a routine with work.

There was conflict brewing in my head, in the hospital, after the hospital, and in the months and years after the shooting. People asked me questions such as, "Do you think he intended to kill you because he shot through the door and he didn't finish it?"

Maybe he didn't mean it, I wondered.

I thought back to when he told me to wrap my wound with the table runner and told me to leave, to go out the door. I had self-talk going on in my head: "Did Tom really mean to do it? Maybe it was an accident. Maybe he only meant to shoot at the lock of the door and not us? Did he? He had all the time in the world to kill us, why didn't he finish it?" It's difficult as a normal, empathetic person to get into the head of someone like Tom, a psychopath. I wanted to normalize it. I wanted to think that maybe it wasn't as bad as I thought. Maybe he did have a moment after William said, "Don't do it Daddy, don't shoot Mommy!" Maybe Tom had a moment of clarity, of "What the fuck did I just do?"

No — I'm not going to give him that. And I never will.

I know at one point during the shooting, he looked out the door and he knew the police were there. He probably thought I was going to die from my wounds anyway. My clothes were covered in blood, he could see I was bleeding out. He was just a coward, not putting the final bullet in me. He was a coward shooting through the door, so he didn't have to look at us. But then, he shot both of us again once he came in. He didn't aim for the head but we were still gravely wounded. So no, there wasn't any thought of, "What have I done? I'm going to save her now and rush over to her side and carry her out." No, he didn't do any of that.

It was a very confusing time. I carried a lot of guilt and even more shame. What if my father had died? Holy shit! I think of my father in the days, weeks, months, and years after the shooting. He could have died because I met that man. I didn't know that would happen. But still, there was guilt.

And also, what if any of those bullets had hit my son? What if Tom killed William? And what if I lived? I would not have been able to function had William died and I lived. If my dad died and I lived, I don't know that I would have been able to bounce back from that either. I don't know that I would have been able to move on as a functioning member of society had either of those scenarios occurred.

I don't think I would have become the fighter I am now, had things turned out differently.

It was a struggle for some time. I know now, yes, he did mean it. You don't show up to your estranged wife's house uninvited with a gun, a knife and backup ammunition. You don't shoot through a door with your family standing behind — estranged or not. I never gave him my address. His intention was to kill. Without a doubt. He had a 9mm Beretta with hollow point bullets to do the most damage.

For the entirety of my relationship with Tom, he continuously preached to all of us: You never point a gun at anyone unless you intend to kill them. He intended to kill us. There we have it, in his own words. The fact that he didn't finish it is irrelevant.

In quiet moments, and also in weaker moments, it was a difficult trauma to rationalize. I felt stupid too. I blamed myself. I went through a time when I thought I was a fucking idiot. "You ignored this red flag Kate, and that red flag Kate." I was able to see all of the early signs so clearly for what they were. Patterns. I thought, normally, a person would know to run. It was as if I was brainwashed or under a spell. It was confusing. It happened systematically and so subtly that I didn't even know what was happening — and then I was in too deep.

And then it became a game of survival.

That was the point when it escalated in Fort Belvoir and then when we moved to Florida. I was a shell of myself. I was trying to get by with two young children. I was frustrated. I was not a stupid person. I was educated. I was strong-willed. I'd had many relationships where I didn't put up with anyone's shit. Even though I dealt with misogyny and patriarchy, a lot of bullshit many women have had to deal with in our lifetimes, I still didn't accept it. I was always opinionated and even mouthy at times. I was a tomboy when I was a kid. I was more masculine than feminine. I wasn't a meek, mousy, weak person that was the stereotype associated with victims of domestic violence.

The fact that I was a victim dogged me. I didn't think it could happen to me. I couldn't believe it.

I had nightmares during the first few years after the shooting. They were never about the shooting itself, or about that trauma. The nightmares were that I was in a relationship with Tom again. There was a foreboding, a confusion. I knew I had to get away from him. He had a distinct look, like I mentioned before — the smug look — and I wanted to run. Then he would smile at me — he would play nice and try to pull me back in but I knew it was fake. Those nightmares had the power to take me off track for the rest of the day. I would wake in a panic attack with my heart racing, thinking I was going to die.

It was interesting that I wasn't affected as much by the physical trauma as I was by the emotional and mental abuse. That was the deeper trauma versus being shot. That was the shit that lingered once the physical wounds healed. It was what I had to dig down deep to unpack with therapy — leaving it as a trail of crumbs and continue on the path. The shooting was the climax of my experience and from then on, my work was to understand everything leading up to it — what I missed and what I didn't know about abuse. I had to take it into my own hands and educate myself.

It has been a long, grueling, on-going journey.

Then in the summer of 2013, the following weekend after the termination of parental rights trial, I had tickets to see the 90s band, 311, with my boyfriend. We were in his car on the way to meet friends, got to the venue, parked, and my phone rang. I didn't recognize the number, but it was a 954 local number to me, and I answered it.

It was a man's voice. "You fucking hit my car!"

"What?" I gasped.

"You destroyed the bumper of my car. You fucking hit my car and left."

"What are you talking about?" I asked.

"I have a gun and I'm going to come get you. I have your address, I know where you are."

I was shaking. I handed the phone over to my boyfriend. He said, "Hello, hello, hello?"

"Fuck you. Fuck you," the man said and hung up.

I went from zero to -250. I melted down. I told my boyfriend to take me home immediately. We did not go to the concert. I called my friend Natasha who was watching Henry and William and asked her to meet me at the police station in Parkland. I told her about the call, convinced it was from Tom, or someone he had hired. We went to the police station to report the incident and their eyes glazed over, as if thinking, "So what? You got a weird call?"

"I'm not fucking around," I said. "He has money, he is capable of hiring someone to kill us. This is a threat."

Then, I thought, "I'm out of here." I called my parents and told them I was booking one-way tickets for the kids and me to Boston, to stay in Rockport and hide.

THIS is PTSD and trauma, folks. Flight mode.

I called my manager at work and told her what happened. She had been through everything with me. She was supportive and told me to take my computer and go — that I could work from there. We literally flew out of Fort Lauderdale the next morning and fled to our safe haven, the family home in Rockport. For the next eight months I remained there. I was safe, I was away from Florida, away from Tom, away from all of it.

To this day, I don't know what that phone call was, if Tom put someone up to it or if it was merely a prank. But it was real to me.

Rockport was my touchstone. I felt safe there. I had family there. It was a small town. Even though officials didn't seem to care about the threatening call or never followed up on it, I needed to take my life in my own hands and do what I could do to feel safe. I regrouped.

In March of 2014, I moved back to Florida. I was ready to achieve normalcy there and reconnect with my people. My parents, my brother and his family were in Florida, my friends and my job were there. I packed up my car with the few belongings I had in Massachusetts, and hit the road south.

But even when I got back there, I still wasn't okay.

William was in regular therapy and doing well, but I still hadn't taken care of myself. I was able to keep it together for another nine or ten months with work and William. I pretended to be normal. I remember being at work and going to lunch with my close coworkers. I would completely disassociate at times. It was like I was up above the scene and looking down, mocking myself. "This is so fake, all of this is bullshit. Listen to what these people are talking about. None of it matters. People are dying. I almost died." I felt like a fraud in my own life.

It all came to a screeching halt in December of 2015.

I was doing a lot of health and wellness blogs at work. I was the regular writer for my company. I had to turn out a lot of content within a month's time. It was the first week of December and I missed the production of two blogs from November. I don't know why I missed them, I just did. I was paralyzed. I couldn't think. I couldn't finish my work. I couldn't focus. It was as if I didn't care. Although I did — I loved my job, I loved my boss. But there was an underlying sensation that I couldn't finish my work. After I missed two blogs, my manager, with concern, asked me about it.

I promised I would scramble and finish them that day. I sat at my computer, pulled up a word document, wrote a title, started to write the first paragraph and I froze. I could feel a wave of panic starting to set in. I was going to lose it — in front of everyone in our open floor space office. There was nowhere for me to go. I quietly packed up my computer, put it in my work bag and shut everything down. I put my bag over my shoulder and without making a scene, I walked out the door. I walked downstairs, to my car, and I began convulsing. I was crying and convulsing and I scared myself. I called my mom and she began to panic. She thought I was going to hurt myself. She said she was sending my dad and in the meantime she stayed on the phone with me.

I messaged my manager and told her I didn't know what was going on but I knew I couldn't continue working. After talking with Human Resources at my company, and learning my options, I decided to engage the Family Leave and Medical Act, which gave me three months off, unpaid. I needed to focus on myself. I wanted my life back. I hated how I felt. I didn't want to let Tom take one more day of my life. He already took too much. It was three years later. Everything came crashing down. My friend did research for me on inpatient and outpatient programs. I was losing my shit. I felt I needed to check in for a month. But I was also conflicted because of Will — he was so young and for me to be away for a month would be hard on him.

We found a program in a neighboring town that did outpatient therapy. It was a four-hour, daily program with cognitive behavioral therapy in a group setting led by a therapist. We found another program that was associated with Nova Southeastern University in Davie — they had a PTSD specific program. I entered the outpatient program and also the PTSD program immediately. I was doing two programs at once. I was determined. I wanted to learn the tools I needed to put myself back together. I wanted to get a handle on my medications, nightmares and triggers. I was dedicated to feeling better.

The outpatient program was Monday through Thursday for four hours. We had group sessions in the morning, followed by lunch. The therapists taught us a variety of skills, and it was very grounding and helpful. There were a lot of hurting people there and it gave me insight into the state of mental health and how we provide for the mentally ill in America. Many of them were refused care after a certain point. And they would have to cycle out even if they were not ready to leave. Many of them came right back in. For me, I needed the self-care. I needed the routine. I needed to care again about my work. Before, all I could think about were people dying and nobody was doing anything about it.

Many of us became close in the group. They were good people going through very difficult times. A lot of them had chronic illnesses. My ex-husband was a psychopath and there was no rehabilitating him. The people that I met at outpatient were good-hearted people who just wanted to get better. It was an eye-opening and moving experience for me. The amount of empathy I received from my group and my therapists was touching. A psychiatrist got my medications on track based on my symptoms. I am glad I did that. Anyone who has suffered from trauma will benefit from realizing the importance of taking the time to get the help you deserve.

The PTSD program was one-on-one with a grad student. He knew trigger exposure. Immediately after the shooting, crowds were a trigger for me. I didn't trust anyone. I was convinced someone would start shooting. So my therapist and I would go to the student union at Nova and sit together. The noise bothered me. The next time we went, he sat at the table near me. The time after that, he sat even further from me. The time after that he sat out of sight. It was about building my confidence and realizing that I was safe. I felt I was taking control over my mental well-being. Was it a cure? No, but all of it working together made a gradual improvement in the quality of my life.

I was off work from December through February, and went back to work in March 2016. I felt stronger. I cycled out of the outpatient program. I cried then, as I had made friends in that group and I loved our therapist. I had a wonderful experience but it was time to move on. I continued to go to PTSD therapy once a week, as it was close to my work.

After all the work I did, I felt strong enough to move back to Alexandria, VA, in the summer of 2016. I was ready to take even more control back. I wanted to be closer to my son Henry, who was living on the Maryland side of DC with his dad. I saw Henry regularly in the years I was in Florida, but I wanted to see him more often. And frankly, I was ready to get out of Florida again, time for a change. Once I knew I had put myself back together, I was ready to move. I began increasing domestic and gun violence advocacy and awareness, and I was much more confident in myself. My move was an effort to fit another piece back together — life in Alexandria with William and Henry.

Chapter 43
The Criminal Trial

When we went in front of one of the judges to finalize the divorce, Tom was there in shackles across the table from me, and the judge was reading over the paperwork. She said to Tom, "You served 25 years in the Air Force?"

"Yes," Tom replied.

"Thank you for your service," the judge continued.

I was sitting there with an oversized brace on my arm that my OT made to support my hand and wrist. I dramatically put my elbow on the table so that my arm and brace were in clear view and glared at the judge. She then looked at me and looked down right away. She realized what she said. It was a knee-jerk response from her. She wasn't thinking of the big picture that this man served 25 years in the Air Force but also attempted to kill his wife and father in law in front of his son. She showed by example the way our country idolized members of the armed services and veterans to hero status. *Perhaps we can turn our attention to the victims?*

In the final phase of the divorce, we had to go back in front of the awful magistrate who said the horrible comments during an earlier proceeding. The entire Broward County Courthouse knew what happened with the Maffei family shooting. We had been through so much with Dependency Court, child services, the divorce, the guardian's ad litem, and several judges and magistrates. I had to go in front of the magistrate with my oversized arm brace and although she was professional, she was visibly uncomfortable. Again, I had to sit across the table from Tom. Every time we had to go to court after the shooting, I was required to sit in close quarters with him. The revictimization was unbelievable. At one point, I was feeling super triggered being in the same space with Tom, his disgusting lawyer and the rude magistrate. I wondered what she thought. I asked if I could go into the other room for the remainder of the hearing because I broke down.

At the point when I broke down, Tom with his shackled hand pushed a box of tissues towards me. I didn't take them. I refused to give him any validation that he could hurt me then swoop in and be my savior again. Screw him — and I told him that with my eyes.

We had negotiated some alimony in lieu of child support because Tom's parental rights were terminated and we wouldn't receive child support for William. The house was also negotiated — I gave it to Tom, which he and his attorney proceeded to rent out for $2,500 a month. That was how he paid his legal fees — in addition to the pension and disability he was still getting from the military.

At the end of the divorce hearing, when we went back into the courtroom, the magistrate made her final statements and we had to sign paperwork. She looked at me and said, "I'm sorry." I looked at her and shook my head. I wasn't going to say it was ok. Instead I said, "I hope everyone learned. I told people he was going to do this." And she looked away.

I want to believe that some of the people involved in that circus were affected by what happened. The truth was that probably, they were not. I felt cynical that they learned anything from the Maffei case. It was a case that was preventable, all the red flags were there, but they all ignored them.

But then we still faced the criminal trial.

When we met with our first prosecutor, she said it was going to take four to five years for the trial. We didn't believe her, but she was right. The years 2013, 2014, 2015 all went by. Continuance after continuance was granted to the defense. We went through three prosecutors. Then 2016 came — and the fourth one was the one who picked it up and carried the ball through trial. Our prosecution team had been right all along, of course. Tom did have more rights than we did. The system didn't care about our closure, they didn't care that we had to wait four years for justice. There was strategy behind the continuances — we didn't want the other side to say they were rushed to trial. Not having enough time to prepare could potentially lead to a set up for a successful appeal. While we understood the continuances, it was still frustrating to experience them.

Every time there was a new trial date, we would receive a subpoena. At first we felt hopeful but after a while we only would glance at it and throw it in a file. Each time the defense would go before a judge and ask for a continuance. That went on for years. It loomed over us. All we could think about was how erratic Florida juries could be. For example, Casey Anthony, a murderer, walked. George Zimmerman, who murdered Trayvon Martin, also walked. There was a lot of anticipation around the trial and what would happen. I knew Tom always got away with everything. He was an Air Force veteran. What if they gave him leniency? He was a white male. He was going to come off as sympathetic. It was a game to him.

We had been deposed in 2015. The first time we almost went to trial was in June 2016, but it was canceled because of the defense's vacation. We almost went to trial another time. Finally, in September 2016, the trial was on. I flew to Florida and wore a "fuck you," black dress. My parents and family, close friends, and a reporter from the *Huffington Post* all were there.

I couldn't eat. I was on the toilet constantly — my stomach was churning non-stop and I felt I was crawling out of my skin. Survivor friends and I call it "court stomach."

When the prosecution began, my dad testified, law enforcement testified and our eye witness testified. The eye witness lived in the apartment directly across from mine. My apartment was ground level and hers was one level up. She could see the entire act unfold through her sliding glass doors. Stacie placed Tom at the scene earlier — he was on the property before I was home from work. Keep in mind that I had only lived in that apartment complex for two weeks. Our eye witness knew enough to take note that she had not seen Tom before. Stacie saw him go up to the door, pull the gun out, shoot it. She heard the screams. Stacie was a nurse and also had a young daughter whom she told to hide under the bed. She called 911. I also learned there was one point when she saw William jumping up and down, screaming, running for the door. Stacie saw Tom pick up William aggressively from behind and carry him back into the apartment and close the door. She was a clutch player. She was a stranger to me before that. But what a strong, brave and credible witness she was.

Soon, I was anticipating my testimony. I couldn't sit still. I was pacing up and down the courtroom hallway. The high level of triggers and anxiety were intolerable. I felt like jumping out of my skin. Waiting to go on the stand against my ex and attempted murderer was indescribable. I was trying to pump myself up inside my head.

Then our victim advocate came out to the hallway. We came to know her well, as she was assigned to us in the beginning and stayed with us through the years. She asked me to sit down.

"There's no easy way to say this," she said. "There's been a mistrial."

It was done. It was over. It had to be rescheduled.

That was the hardest gut-punch ever. I collapsed into myself. My friends came out and hugged me, followed by my mom. We were crying and hugging each other. Then we went back into the courtroom to hear what the judge would say.

After the lead detective testified, before it was my turn to go on the stand, the court took a recess. Our prosecutors were deciding whether to put me on the stand at that point — they didn't want to feel rushed since it was later in the afternoon. They were thinking about starting with my testimony the next morning. When they came back from recess, they actually were preparing to put me on the stand. Then one of the jurors passed a note to the judge, asking if they would be able to hear the jailhouse tape between Tom and his mother the night of the shooting because it was difficult to hear. However, the jurors were not supposed to be talking to each other about the case at all until it was time for deliberations. So legally, the mistrial was born.

The judge admonished the jury — they failed and had not followed instructions. It was their fault that the trial was ending. The entire debacle was extremely frustrating and heart breaking. None of it went the way we thought it should have gone.

Once the jury was released, the attorneys consulted their calendars with the judge. They settled on a November date. Again, the November date came and I received a call from our victim advocate that the trial date would need to be postponed again — to January 2017. We were pretty confident the trial would not proceed then either, as it was to start the day after the New Year and holiday break.

So the January date came and I received a call again. That time the defense attorney told the judge he needed more time to prepare, since he had been away during the holidays. The trial was postponed — again — to February.

Everyone assured us that it was absolutely happening in February and nothing would get in the way. We chuckled to ourselves. We would believe it when the trial was over!

Well, we did go to trial in February 2017. My childhood friend flew down from New Jersey. My brother and sister-in-law, my parents, my uncle, my best friend and her daughter — there was a large group of people to support us. A brand new jury was selected and apparently that time the judge was extremely clear on what the jury could and could not do, to prevent another mistrial. The same order of testimonies took place.

They played the jailhouse tape.

Tom's mother was talking to him: "Tommy are you ok, are you eating ok? Are you making friends?"

As if he was away at fucking camp.

"The story just doesn't make any sense, Tommy," she questioned him.

"Mom I was just trying to shoot at the lock of the door cause Kate was trying to keep me out. I shot three times at the lock," Tom countered.

Meanwhile, the photographs from the scene show three body mass shots, right through the middle of the door.

"That doesn't really make any sense, Tommy. Tommy, don't you remember a couple years ago when you sat at my kitchen table and said 'if I find her, I'll kill her?' " she asked.

Tom jumbled some unintelligible words together in response. At another point in the tape, Tom told his mom that they were being recorded and she couldn't say all of those things. He was sunk and he knew it.

There was also a revelation of a Google search on Tom's phone: husband killing wife. He had pulled up a couple videos, which proved premeditation. It wasn't a crime of passion. He didn't just snap. He showed up with extra ammunition and he had a hunting knife on him.

Then I went on the stand. I was prepared, I was advised on what to expect but it was still as scary as hell. I wanted the jury to empathize with the terror I experienced. I also did not want to be judged like women often are for being in an abusive relationship. *Did Kate do something to make Tom shoot her?* There was a lot of uncertainty swirling through my head.

The most impactful part of being on the stand was when the court played the 911 tape for me from start to finish. I sobbed through the entire call. I looked at my mother and she was doubled over while listening. My friends were holding her. It was a very long audio. It was one of the most horrific 911 tapes I'd ever heard, *and it was my own.* To hear my own voice as I begged Tom, as I screamed. Tom was yelling and that triggered me. The 911 operator was trying to figure out what the hell was going on.

At one point I looked over at the jury and a couple of the men had tears in their eyes, one with tears streaming down his face and they were glaring at Tom. Then they looked at me — almost in disbelief that I was still alive. Tom gave little reaction while hearing the lengthy 911 tape. He rotated between a blank expression and a smug one. He was probably proud of himself. He probably loved hearing the fear in my voice again.

The defense questioned me more about Tom's mental state and the medications he took. He wasn't in any type of therapy that I was aware of, I told them. They continuously brought up PTSD from his military experience — although Tom never experienced combat while serving in the military. Tom's attorney lied — or Tom lied to his attorney. In the opening and closing statements, they stated Tom was in a Humvee explosion in Iraq. Tom was never in Iraq. They painted a false narrative of a war hero. Tom claimed the injuries he received from his motorcycle accident were from the imaginary Humvee explosion. Tom was never deployed to Iraq or Afghanistan and the fact that Tom's lawyer made reference to that to stimulate empathy for him was disgusting.

They also had an absurd claim of "involuntary intoxication." The claim was that Tom was suffering from depression and anxiety, went to the VA hospital earlier in the day of the shooting and was prescribed Klonopin for anxiety. They claimed that he either took too much of it or didn't follow the directions and had an adverse reaction that caused him to try to murder us.

That was their defense.

There was a psychologist who met with Tom for about three hours during the time leading up to the trial. The doctor had never treated Tom before or given him medications and didn't know much about his past medical history. He didn't know he took Klonopin before — and I know he did, he took it when we were married.

At the end of the day, our prosecutor, shredded the defense. She asked the psychologist how much he was getting paid for his testimony. My friends and family filled me in about much of these details. I wasn't allowed to be in the courtroom for that testimony because I was a witness.

We were all expecting Tom to go on the stand next.

After the prosecution tore apart the psychologist's testimony, the defense took a recess, then came back and rested their case. Our victim advocate rushed out and let us know that Tom was not going on the stand, that they'd rested.

I think our prosecutor was a bit disappointed that Tom didn't go on the stand because she was ready to light him on fire. She was ready to go. I also would have liked to have heard all about that — a strong woman destroying him on the stand. But that's okay. It's probably better he never had a chance to lie through his teeth.

The jury was sent into deliberation. My group of family and friends went to lunch — we were discussing all points, especially about the psychiatrist getting ripped apart. We went back to the courtroom around 3 p.m. to wait with our prosecutors. It turned out to be several hours of waiting while they deliberated. It was bizarre that Tom and his lawyer also were waiting in the same courtroom. Our bench was within earshot of Tom. I made some comments under my breath but loud enough for him to hear. "Loser, fuck you." Tom was visibly uncomfortable. He couldn't do much, he couldn't surf on a phone. He pretended to sift through trial papers and such, avoiding looking in our direction.

I was there with all my people. Tom had nobody, not even his mother. Nobody. His own attorney didn't seem to like him. At one point during the wait, he was sitting next to Tom at the defense table but announced he was going to move across the room. He joked with the prosecutors and even came over to interact with us. Such an odd experience.

It took longer than anticipated. There were several counts and the jury has to consider each count and go through a checklist process. It went on for several hours. Finally, around 8:30 p.m., the verdict was in, and the jury was ushered to the courtroom. The judge greeted them and asked if they came to a verdict — they said "yes."

We were all holding hands, squeezing together, already emotional.

"We the jury, find the defendant guilty on all counts."

My family and friends cheered and hugged. I looked over at Tom. He refused to look at me.

FINALLY THEY DIDN'T BUY TOM'S BULLSHIT!!!

The judge and attorneys looked at their calendars and set a sentencing date for another couple of months, in April. Yes, he was found guilty on everything, but the sentencing was up to the judge. Nonetheless, we had relief. That murderous, abusive fucker had been found GUILTY!

After the verdict was delivered, it was time to leave the courtroom. There were cameras and media waiting in the hallway. Our double-attempted murder trial was definitely newsworthy. When I saw the cameras, I beamed and I put my arms up in victory and yelled, "Yeah!"

They came over to us and held microphones up. My dad and I talked and expressed how relieved we were that justice had been served. I said my victory was for all women who experienced abuse. It happens too often and I would continue fighting for them.

Following the trial, we took time to write our victim impact statements before the sentencing. I wrote one, my dad did, my mom did, my now-ex-boyfriend wrote one, and I helped William write one.

On sentencing day in April, my mom, dad and I read our statements in front of the judge. We pleaded for life without parole. All said and done, Tom received 60 years in prison without a chance to get out. He was 49 at the time, so the math talks.

He will die in prison.

He won't see the light of day again. Our society and women are better for it. We fought. We didn't let up and he was held accountable for his actions. With everything that occurred during the judicial process, we were fortunate it ended with the results it did, thanks to our due diligence.

Chapter 44
Agony To Advocacy

From my hospital bed, I made the decision that somehow and in some way I would scream my story from the rooftops. I was not sure if it was the fighter instinct within me or something else. I was angry with Tom, with the police, and with the court system. I was like, "No, none of this is okay. I want people to know. HE did this to US."

I'm a writer. I thought maybe I would blog about it. Some of my friends asked my permission and put together a public Facebook page, called "Love & Support for Kate Ranta and Family." Now, it is called, "Kate Ranta, Survivor Inspired Speak Up (SISU)." "Sisu" in Finnish — my heritage — means strength, resilience, perseverance, courage, and bravery. I now have the word tattooed on my right wrist just under the scar where I was shot.

The Facebook page originally was a way for people to stay informed with what was happening with us, and send support and words of encouragement. When I got home from the hospital, I immediately took over the page and wanted to share my journey. I posted photos of the shooting, my injured hand, and photos of William and me with my family. I posted what I was going through, my thoughts, feelings and frustrations, all of it. I explained what happened and how we arrived at the place we were.

NBC Miami picked up my story and came to my house to interview me about five days after the shooting and that was the first time I entertained any media attention. We were told from the start, from the prosecutors, that we were not to talk to the media. Something in me said, "screw that." I chose to do what I wanted, what felt right to me. I did some media early on and continued with the public Facebook page, which went viral at one point. It started with a couple hundred friends and family until another survivor page found mine and began to promote me. Their followers joined in and I watched it grow to several thousand.

When I first started sharing on the public page, I thought if I could save one life, it would be worth it. If my story could influence and encourage one woman to get out of an abusive relationship, then I would be happy I had done my job. That goal came to fruition only six months later when a woman contacted me via a private message through my page. She was 25 years old and in an emotionally abusive relationship with a military guy. She connected with my story. She was also very afraid that the violence could happen to her. Through talking with her, she developed the strength to leave the marriage. At the time, she was stationed with her husband in Ohio, but her mother lived in Coral Springs, Florida of all places. Approximately a year or two later, once she moved and started a new life, she visited her mother in Coral Springs. I invited her to my parents' house. She hugged me and thanked me. We are still friends today. I love that I'm still in contact with the first woman my story impacted.

Then one woman became — not enough. I knew I wanted to keep going.

As it turned out, the Sandy Hook Elementary School shooting took place six weeks after I was shot. My friends advised us not to turn on the news. Our injuries were literally still raw. I didn't watch the actual footage but I knew what happened. In the aftermath of that a new gun control group was founded. I knew a little about it, but in February 2014, a good, long-time friend texted me about an acquaintance who was working for the organization — Moms Demand Action for Gun Sense in America. I talked with her and told her my story and she immediately brought me into the fold. And that was how I joined what is called the "gun violence prevention movement."

I found out that when I was on the right path, the universe kept me moving on it.

In the beginning it was Moms Demand Action For Gun Sense in America and Mayors Against Illegal Guns, which Mayor Michael Bloomberg of New York City established years before. They were folding together to create Everytown for Gun Safety. I was in the first commercial for the launch of Everytown. It was to be gun control's answer to the National Rifle Association (NRA). I started doing more advocacy with them. They created a survivor network and fellowship, and I was involved in the first class. I had numerous media opportunities over the years including being featured in the *Huffington Post* and *Rolling Stone Magazine*. William and I were on the JumboTron in Times Square for the Wear Orange Campaign to support gun violence prevention. I also was part of a gun violence video series Spike Lee created to air during the National Basketball Association (NBA) Finals.

Our story has been featured in two documentaries: Brave New Films', *Making A Killing: Guns, Greed & the NRA,* directed by Robert Greenwald, as well as *Finding Jenn's Voice,* directed by Tracy Schott. Seeing the story at viewings on big screens and participating as part

206 • KILLING KATE

of panel discussion afterwards — have had real power to affect change.

When I first moved back to Virginia in 2016, I was asked to speak on the steps of the U.S. Capitol with Speaker of the United States House of Representatives Nancy Pelosi and U.S. Representative John Lewis. We were surrounded by advocates, activists and supportive House Democrats. I stood on a wall in front of the United States Capitol the night before and shouted our story to the clapping and cheering crowd — that was when House Dems had a sit-in. Will joined me in all of that. We were side by side. I spoke at a rally after the mass shooting in the Pulse, a gay nightclub in Orlando in 2016. It was there that Will spoke as well. I leveraged my story anywhere and everywhere. I took any and all opportunities to get my story out and helped create awareness that domestic gun violence happens to real people. I wanted to shatter stereotypes, show the reality.

The advocacy work was energizing and empowering. It has never been about notoriety — it has always been about telling my story and creating change through awareness. I want to believe that eventually it will hit the right ears. We can actually make concrete steps toward change.

There came a time when I felt let down by Everytown. It was when I and other survivors learned about their partnership with the Fraternal Order of Police. It is a racist and awful police organization that also had just supported Donald Trump for President. Some of us discussed how police brutally has resulted in the murders of African Americans and we weren't ok with that. "You're going to partner with a group that calls a 12-year-old boy a 'thug'?" No, we didn't feel that was okay at all. Some of us spoke up and Everytown didn't like it. We were kicked out of the survivor network and fellowship. And so began my stronghold on finding strength in my voice — and using it even if it meant being cast out. I didn't feel free to share my message the way I wanted to. I had evolved as a survivor, as a person, and as a strong woman. I wanted to say words such as, "gun control" and "gun reform" and I felt controlled as to what I could and couldn't say when involved within the organization.

Now, I'm a gun violence survivor on my own terms, and pick and choose where I want to be involved. I'm not exclusive to any one organization, and when I can help, I'm willing to do it. I'm going to continue pushing forward. I'm in the epicenter, in Washington D.C. I have opportunities to continue getting the message out.

It's important to note that I was extremely enthusiastic to advocate in the beginning. I think that's normal for a survivor — I wanted others to understand what happened to me. I wanted to do anything and everything I could. And for a long time, I ceased to take part in self-care after sharing my story or participating in events. I told my story, then it was time to go home, and then I had to reset myself back into the regular world. When survivors become involved in advocacy, they have to practice kindness and care for themselves more than ever. They have to take the time to decompress after events, see their therapist, or engage in caring for themselves in whatever way works. In the moment, it feels exhilarating, but there is the potential to crash after an event is done and everyone goes home. It's known as "survivor burnout." Sharing can be retraumatizing and retriggering. At times, I occasionally underestimated the after-effects. I'd be irritable and snappy, and then ask myself what was going on? Even if it was a couple days later, I realized that I didn't have a self-care plan in place.

I want to encourage all survivors to harness the strength to speak out. Especially with domestic abuse — there is so much shame and blame involved. Multiple times, people have asked if Tom was drunk or on drugs. Followed by, "What did you do to make him snap? You must have been cheating." People want to blame the woman and look for a reason that made the man act the way he did. More women speaking out and telling their truths specifically about intimate partner violence will create the catalyst for change.

Many women's stories I've heard are eerily similar to mine. Not all details are the same but the way they unfold is similar and the men's behaviors are similar. Wouldn't it be great if there was a database where women could go in and enter their stories to provide a data collection and blow the lid off domestic abuse? There is a pattern in their behavior, and the escalation follows a predictable pattern also. The hurt and the abuse is preventable. The longer we hide in shame, the longer this epidemic will continue to be a problem in our society. We need emotional and mental abuse, all forms of abuse, brought out from the shadows to enlighten the stigma.

The only way to blast that top off is by women speaking out.

Chapter 45
The Appeal

Before the trial even started, we were informed that defendants always file for an appeal, regardless if it is a slam-dunk case or not. That goes back to the importance of taking time to prepare for the trial to ensure there will be no grounds for a successful appeal. As expected, Tom's criminal attorney informed the media they would file an appeal right away. We were told not to worry about it, our victim advocate would keep us updated on the appeal.

The trial took place in February 2017, the sentencing followed in April and the appeal was held in June 2018. We received notice that Tom's attorney would appear in front of an Appellate Court in West Palm Beach, fighting for an appeal. We had confidence that there was no likelihood that Tom was getting out. In the original trial, the judge was fair, not biased. The jury agreed with the prosecution, did their due diligence, deliberated fairly and convicted Tom. We knew that everything followed the books — but it was still scary. What if one of the three judges on the Appellate Court was sexist or an abuser himself?

It felt scary that there was even a sliver of a chance the conviction would be overturned and we would have to go to trial again. In the days leading up to the appeal and during the trial, I experienced "court stomach" again. My anxiety was ultra-high. I worked from home that week to have flexibility to watch the appeal, live streamed via the West Palm Beach Courthouse website.

There was an attorney general assigned to represent the state in the appeal, whom we never met. We felt we didn't have any control. We worried she would not be as invested in us, our story, or our family as our prosecution team was. We were just names on a paper. We had to trust she would represent us to the best of her ability and the outcome would remain in our favor.

Not surprising, the appeal proved to be a real shit show. It felt vindicating to watch it. I signed onto the portal to live stream and when it started I turned on my Facebook Live. 1 felt exhilarated by the support, watching many of my friends join me in viewing it. They were sending emoji reactions and posting messages of support to me and my family.

Tom's attorney lied again about the Humvee explosion and made more excuses about Tom's medications. I thought I wanted to throw my laptop. It still just pisses me off so much that he could make those false claims and not be checked. Then the attorney general had a turn and made a strong argument that everything had proceeded correctly in the trial. She claimed that nothing excused what the defendant did. As with everything else up to that date, they didn't have a ruling right after the appeal ended. Our victim advocate told us it could be a month of wait time before hearing a decision. Actually, it came back within a week. The appeal was denied. They upheld the decision by our trial judge.

Our next question was: How many times could Tom appeal? The answer: Apparently, he could appeal all the way to the Supreme Court. However, at that point I assumed Tom was out of money. I didn't think his lawyer would be up for another appeal after the first was denied. What argument would he make for the second go round? If Tom did file another appeal, however, it wouldn't have surprised me. It would be another example of how the court system is lenient towards defendants and perpetrators. A jury found him guilty based on the facts and evidence. The judge made his determination based on the jury's decision along with the facts and evidence of the case as well. Yet, Tom could appeal. The appeal was denied. And he could appeal again and again? How about he did it, and he's paying the price — end of story?

I do feel much more confident now with the outcome of the trial, and the outcome of the appeal. And even if he appeals again? Tom is screwed.

After Tom went into the Florida prison system, I signed up for Vine Link app, which alerts victims if there is any movement regarding the prisoner, such as if he is in the hospital or if he's moved to a different prison.

After the appeal, they did move Tom from one prison to another in Florida, and that felt rattling. What if he had an escape plan? What if he was able to overpower the guards? Those were the thoughts that went through my head as a victim. Going through a debacle like that, nothing was far-fetched. I didn't put anything past him. I got an alert when he went into the hospital. This guy often went to the hospital and he lied about having cancer before. Because of HIPPA laws, we did not receive any information on why he was in the infirmary. A friend of mine did some research and discovered that the infirmary was located on the prison campus. It was a relief once I discovered he was moved from the infirmary to the new prison location.

People often assume that I have relief and don't feel anxious anymore now that Tom is behind bars. The truth is, I will never feel completely safe as long as Tom is alive. He doesn't have a hold on me — he doesn't have that power. It was the trauma and PTSD I experienced, with their lasting effects. Tom is a sneaky, scary, and a dangerous man. Like I said before, the nightmares I've had are not about the shooting. They are about being back in a relationship with him again. The fact that Tom is in prison, doesn't provide me with complete security. Maybe with time it will fade. I continue to have times where I feel cautious, where I look over my shoulder. Sometimes I get into my car and quickly check the backseat to ensure no one is there. It's difficult to live with the level of trauma I experienced and feel normal. I have a new normal now.

I continue to heal. I continue to evolve. I am in a better place.

Chapter 46
Pieces Of The
Puzzle

I connected with Tom's ex-wives after the shooting. His wife before me would not respond to my messages on Facebook when I attempted to contact her after I left him, but before the shooting. Once Tom was convicted, I sent her the media and she did respond. I had a rush of adrenaline once I realized she was actually going to talk with me. We met over dinner and had a three-hour-long data dump of everything Tom had done to both of us. What he did to her, he also did to me — to a science. With two exceptions.

One was that Tom was physically abusive to her, starting two weeks after they married. They also had a quick engagement and married quickly after a trip to Mexico. Probably even the same resort Tom took me to. He also built a brand new house with her in Ohio, where they were stationed. On one level it felt offensive — as if I was not unique in any way. But in another way, it also was a relief. Once I was awakened to him and remembered Tom bragging about stalking his ex, I realized he lied about everything. He lied about her cheating and he probably did try to kill her too. He was crazy.

I also learned that when she left Tom, she had to return with police, just like I did, to retrieve her things. She moved to an undisclosed apartment, but he found her and stalked her there. What he bragged about to me — breaking into her car, stealing the stereo system and GPS from her car was true, she confirmed that. He terrorized her. When they were married, he would hit her in places that were not visible, or if they were, she would have to cover them up. The military was not helpful to her. She had to obtain a civilian restraining order. Her commander and his commander did nothing to assist her, they only protected Tom. One may think the military protects their own. They protect their own only if they have a penis. If you don't have a penis, you're screwed.

After the end of their relationship, I believe he was stalking online dating sites for his new victim — I was the chosen one. I took the attention off her. He had a new prey to play with.

She also shared that their divorce was final in April 2008.

Tom and I got married in March 2008.

Before we went to Vegas, Tom was telling me of a glitch in the courthouse system with his divorce. Some paperwork wasn't filed properly due to negligence with the system and he wasn't actually divorced. But before we boarded that flight to Vegas to get married, he claimed he fixed it.

But no, their divorce wasn't final for another month, and I believed her. The entire time I was living with him, engaged to him, became pregnant with our child, he was still technically married to her. He knew he was screwed when we made the arrangements to get married in Vegas in March. He apparently thought he could wing it and get away with it.

So technically my marriage to Tom was invalid. He was still married to another woman. His divorce was not finalized when I married him.

I also messaged with another ex-wife, who I actually didn't know was a wife until after our marriage ended. He'd talked about her, but claimed they'd only lived together.

No. He'd married her. It only lasted a year.

He'd met her online as well — she was a single mom. She said he seemed to be okay when they lived in North Dakota, but when Tom was transferred to Ohio, he brought her with him. According to what Tom told me, he kicked her out because she wouldn't work. However, of course he was lying. He was emotionally abusive and one time physical, so she actually bailed after one year of their marriage. I didn't even know they were married!

Another lie.

His first wife, he met in Germany where he was stationed when he was 19. I don't know anything about that marriage, as I've not been able to find her. They were together for 10 years though, so I can only imagine what she went through with him.

His behavior seemed to escalate with each new relationship.

I believe that in addition to giving me Ambien when fracturing my foot, he gave it to me at other times and violated me. It was a pattern in his previous relationships. There were many times after we got back together when I would black out and Tom would tell me it was from wine, but I didn't drink that much and I felt completely out of it the next day.

I realized that was Tom's pattern with many women. I wasn't alone. In surviving the shooting and getting Tom sent to prison for the rest of my life, a psychopath is now off the streets and he can no longer victimize more women. It stopped with me. That feels refreshing. Not a lot of women get to take their abusers off the streets, away from society and other women. There is not another woman after me who will have to experience what I did with him.

And if there was, she most likely would have died quickly. It's a major victory.

He lost. He fucked with the wrong woman.

I love that I survived. I love that my family has been a strong and supportive team. I love that we were vigilant in our demands with the court system. I love that we were persistent in our demands for justice. I love and admire the woman I became throughout the process.

Chapter 47
The Bond Between Us

My family really pulled together after the shooting. It was tough on all of us. My father struggled in the aftermath, trying to discern how the red flags went past without an intervention in our marriage. When I began to blog, speak out and advocate, I think it actually began to help my dad understand and fully process what happened to me. Both of my parents are supportive and we've had to process and educate ourselves together. Even after the shooting, I was still uninformed about the signs and patterns of emotional abuse. I wasn't an expert or schooled in domestic abuse.

Now I am. No degree necessary.

Together, we worked on the Brave New Films documentary. My parents were involved in the filming. They were open and honest, not shy about being interviewed. They've been there with me through all my advocacy. In the beginning, they were concerned. Being rule-followers, our family was honest to a fault and the prosecutor advised us not to talk to media and there I was — talking to the media. Filming a documentary! Exactly what I was advised not to do. I became a rule-breaker after the shooting. I found power in using my voice. There were police reports that said Tom shot me. I felt confident my case would not be affected by speaking out and telling the truth.

I know many survivors who are shamed and blamed by their families. They may be estranged by their parents or siblings and I am so thankful that my friends and family rallied around me. I am fortunate to have the people in my life that I have.

William and I have continued therapy through the years. Will's anxiety after the shooting has been centered around me. He's been afraid he will lose me. Before the shooting, Will always slept in his own bed, in his own room. However since the shooting, he has not been able to sleep alone. He is now 10. There are bigger battles to fight. That's not one I care to fight. I want him to feel safe at all times.

We rescued our dog, Tuukka, in December 2014. I got her because I wanted some form of protection and read about dogs being a danger deterrent for women living alone and single moms. Tuukka is very protective of her people. She will go after someone who would attempt to hurt us. A year ago, I adopted two cats, Mushi and Mio who are 14, living out their golden years with us. Will and Mio share a special bond.

When we were still living in Florida, Will was ultra-vigilant about men, in general. If we were out in public and a man looked at me, Will didn't like it and would walk in front of me or walk closely next to me and glare at the man, as if to fend him off. He was 6 years old but he was prepared to fight off any man who came close to me. Our roles were reversed. Will felt he had to take on the role as protector of me, even though that is typically the role of the parent. It became intense at times. One day I was walking Tuukka and she was taking longer than normal to go to the bathroom. As I was walking up the driveway to my parents' house, I saw Will standing in the window shaking and sobbing uncontrollably. I went inside and asked him what was wrong. He told me, "I thought you were dead! You were gone too long."

I explained that Tuukka was just taking a long time but Will's anxiety reached a high level and if he couldn't see me or if I didn't return quickly, he feared I could be dead. I worked with Will for several years to lower his anxiety with concern for my safety. I've told him I am tough. My body took two bullets and I didn't die. No one will mess with me again. "Mommy's got this." Will has PTSD just as my dad and I do. It has affected Will's school work and his motivation.

Last year, I had a realization, when Will was in third grade. I was talking with his therapist and asked if we should screen him for ADHD. The teachers continued to comment on Will's lack of motivation. We realized it was a PTSD symptom. I struggle with it too and notice it when I am at work. Focus is difficult. Caring about the work can be tough. Why would it be any different for William?

I advocated for him to obtain a 504 Plan program at school, to allow him special accommodations in the classroom for testing and for homework. I also learned about opting him out of the standardized testing in Virginia. I want Will to be a good person and a good man, and that is what matters to me. It is ok with me if he is an average student. That's not where I put my focus on parenting him.

My parents have started advocating on their own. They have their own fire burning now. We also recently celebrated their 50th wedding anniversary. My brother and I threw a surprise party for them in August 2018. It was emotional. There was a chance my mom could have been alone on her 50th wedding anniversary. There was a chance her daughter and her grandson wouldn't have been there either. As a family, we no longer take milestones and special occasions for granted. Every holiday, every birthday, every milestone is celebrated and revered as a gift. There were almost people missing — forever — and no family should have to experience that. But we are strong and we are always going to be there for each other. A monster tried to come between us. He tried hard, but he didn't accomplish it.

There is something very special about the Rantas. We are genuine people. I am blown away by the fact that bullets were shot through a door with three human beings standing on the other side of it. Two were shot twice and all three of us lived through it. It's not something that happens. Most of the time, someone who experiences that is no longer around. There was a good chance my voice could have been silenced. But I lived.

And my voice is stronger than ever.

And that is why I'm on a mission to tell my story.

Amazingly, three hours had passed by since Kate and I began talking.

I looked at Kate with this mixture of shock, camaraderie, and a yearning — a pull that her story had to be told in its entirety — and shared with the world.

We both had tears in our eyes. In that moment, I knew in my soul... there was an unidentifiable bond between us.

Her voice was shaky at times as she was filled with emotion from reliving the red flags she missed, the trauma she endured and yet — I saw this bold, irrepressible spirit to survive. It was a recipe I admired. I had to know more.

"Kate, have you thought about writing your own book?" I asked. "I can help you write your story — and help you tell it in the way you want it to be told."

I left our meeting, and took an Uber to the airport, when this text came across my phone:

Killing Kate
Acknowledgements

First, I would like to acknowledge Alisa Divine, my co-author, for her help in making this book happen — we've been quite a team; and to Dr. Thomas Haller for empowering us from day one to bring my story to the public. I would also like to thank Evan Rachel Wood and Lovern Gordon for their respective contributions with the foreword and the introduction — I appreciate your love, light and support.

I'd like to acknowledge the following people who played parts big and small in this journey. I could not have made it this far without your love, support, encouragement, hard work, dedication, and so much more:

My parents, Robert & Susan Ranta; my son, William Ranta, who witnessed the shooting; my son, Henry Williams, who thankfully was not there; my brother, Matt Ranta, his wife Lauren, and nephews Brian & Justin; my uncle, Steve Ranta, who *always* has my back.

Dear, close, long-time friends — Kent & Connie Sadar, Jennifer Pirchio, Erin Hardtke, Kaysha Johnston, Valerie Gregory, Rachael Joseph, Casey Musselman — who dropped everything to be there for my family and me through the years in so many ways.

Santiago Paez, who was there at the shooting and there for me afterward; extended family Jane Phillips, Amy Jordan, Jessi and Lily Lorenzo; long-time Ranta family friends Cozzis, Giebases, Inginos, Judy Delahunty, Rita Meehan; the Olson family in Rockport.

My manager and friend at Solstice Benefits, Alissa Gavrilescu, COO Carlos Ferrera, and wonderful Solstice friends who became like family.

So many kick ass and courageous survivor sisters I've met along the way, as well as gun violence prevention advocates and activists in the fight I've met along the way — too many to list but you know who you are.

My divorce attorney, Bonnie Canty and paralegal, Maura Rolls, who showed empathy and worked tirelessly for us.

Parkland BSO Dep. Lou Marchese; BSO Child Investigator Shanitrice Sims; Coral Springs Det. Chris Collins; our first responders in Coral Springs who kept us alive.

Our prosecution team Molly McGuire and Whitney Makay; our original prosecutor Katya Pitman; victim advocate Suzy Mattson-Brown; Judge Raj Singhal; eyewitness Tracy Scott; our jury in Broward County who found him guilty; the attorney general who tried the Termination of Parental Rights trial and won!

Discovery Preschool teachers Jessica Lefkowitz and Irene Kelly, director Miss Penny, and Discovery staff for unbelievable love toward William; Discovery School moms for food and tuition support; Park Trails Elementary Kindergarten teacher, Robyn Clark, for making William's transition to elementary school beautiful.

Our amazing occupational therapist Heidi Lipshutz who got my hand moving again and became a friend along the way; therapists at Henderson Behavioral Health, University-Pavilion Behavioral Health, Trauma Resolution Integration Program — Nova Southeastern who treated William and me.

Brave New Films Director Robert Greenwald, for featuring our story in *Making A Killing: Guns, Greed and the NRA*; Director Tracy Schott-Wagner, for featuring our story in *Finding Jenn's Voice*; and Senior Reporter Melissa Jeltson, of the *Huffington Post*, for tireless and accurate reporting on domestic and gun violence.

Facebook and social media supporters, GoFundMe contributors — strangers I don't even know but who've shown support.

U.S. Congressman Ted Deutch, of Florida, and U.S. Senator Chris Murphy, of Connecticut, who have been strong supporters of my family and me, and who have been fighting for gun reform and standing up to the NRA for years.